It Is Simply All About Them*

* The clients!

Learn why some consultants are more effective than others

Norman S. Wei

Published in the United States by
Environmental Management and Training LLC.
P.O. Box 152239
Cape Coral, FL 33915

ISBN-13: 978-1475139693

COPYRIGHT © 2012 by Norman S. Wei. ALL RIGHTS RESERVED

Reproduction or translation of any part of this work beyond that permitted by Section 107 or 108 of the 1976 United States Copyright Act without the permission of the copyright owner is unlawful. Requests for permission for further information should be addressed to Norman Wei, Environmental Management and Training LLC. P.O. Box 152239, Cape Coral FL 33915.

This publication is sold with the understanding that the publisher is not engaged in rendering legal, accounting, or other professional services. If legal advice or other expert assistance is required, the services of a competent professional person should be sought.

Table of Contents

Preface and Introduction 1

Chapter 1: What Really Goes on Inside the "New" Corporation 5

    How Do Companies Select Consultants? 7

    Is Cost the Real Determining Factor? 9

Chapter 2: How to Approach Your Future Clients 15

    The Issue of Prices 16

    What Should You Emphasize In Your Sales Pitch 19

    Always Focus on Your Strength and Project the Right Image 21

    The Uniquely Qualified and Full Service Firms 24

    Selling Your Services - the Basics 25

Chapter 3: Listening to Your Future Clients 29

    The Art of Active Listening 29

    Always Look for High Quality Information 32

    Asking Open-ended Questions 40

    Asking the Right Questions 47

    A Meeting With Bad Outcome 52

A Meeting With Good Outcome 53

An Analysis of the two meetings 55

The Doctor-Patient Model 56

How to deal with conference calls with your clients 57

Chapter 4:   Marketing in the Internet Age 61

Visit Your Future Client's Website 61

Key Points about Your Website 62

Make Use of Social Media 65

Email Handling Etiquettes 67

Chapter 5: Making Sales Presentations 71

Making Your Ideas Stick 75

Preparing for the Presentation 77

Delivering the Presentation 81

Handling Questions during the Presentation 84

Chapter 6: Special Tips on Making PowerPoint Presentations 87

PowerPoint as a Visual Tool 89

Open with Five Slides 93

The Three Main Points of Presentation 94

The Vioxx Story (non-bullet points in action) 98

Why PowerPoint Makes Us Stupid? 103

Key points about PowerPoint Presentation 105

Handling nervousness during the presentation 124

Chapter 7: Selling to a Selection Committee 129

   A Few Words about Politics 130

Chapter 8: To Bid or Not to Bid 133

Chapter 9: Submitting Proposals 141

   Preparing unsolicited Proposals 142

Chapter 10: How to Write Winning Proposals 145

   Developing a Theme 145

   Responding to the RFP 146

   Meeting Internal Deadlines 150

   Writing Style 150

   Cost Analysis 152

   Murphy's Law 154

   Anatomy of a successful proposal 155

Chapter 11: How to Protect Your Proposal 159

Chapter 12: Working With Regulatory Agencies 163

Chapter 13: Thirteen Common Mistakes Made by Consultants 169

Mistake #1: Fail to Return All Phone Calls Promptly 171

Mistake #2: Change Orders 175

Mistake #3: Wanting Extra for High Quality Product 177

Mistake # 4: Fail to Learn Your Trade 179

Mistake # 5: Prepare Dishonest Proposals 183

Mistake # 6: Fail to Project a Positive and Right Image 185

Mistake #7: Fail to Maintain a Personal Touch 189

Mistake #8: Lack of Passion 191

Mistake #9: Fail to Provide Service with a Smile 193

Mistake #10: Promising Too Much and Delivering Less 195

Mistake# 11: Fail to Keep Their Existing Clients Happy 199

Mistake #12: Fail to Do Those Little Things 203

Mistake #13: Fail to Deal with Complaints Promptly 205

Additional References 207

About the Author 211

In-House Seminars by Norman Wei 213

Preface and Introduction

This is not your usual book.

This is a book for consultants and people who plan to hire consultants.

In this book, the author shares his insights on how consultants are actually selected - from the inside perspective of a corporate buyer/client. As a corporate manager for a Fortune 500 company, he hired and fired numerous consultants and contractors. He provides specific case studies of how some consultants are successful in being selected and why others are much less successful.

The rather unusual aspect of this book is that the author has also been a consultant. So he speaks from both sides of the table.

This book contains material used in training seminars. One of the features is a discussion of 13 most common mistakes made by many consultants.

The term "consultant" used in this book refers to anyone who offers his or her professional services to companies and general public. This includes engineers, architects, accountants, attorneys, realtors, contractors, plumbers, electricians, etc. The terms "client" and "future client" are used interchangeably throughout the book because the same care and efforts you spend to convert a future client into a client should be continued in order to keep the client.

> "The customer is the lifeblood of your organization, so give them all you've got, for without them, you've got nothing! It is simply all about them!"
>
> Tom Peters

This book offers some no-holds-barred and take-no-prisoner advice on dealing with this new reality. The name of the game is to make connection with your future and existing clients. This is also a self-critical look at the consulting industry from the perspective of a professional who has worked on both sides – as a consultant as well as a buyer of professional services.

The focus of this book is on an approach that places your clients before you. You take care of your clients and your service will sell itself. You listen to your future clients' needs first and you will be able to sell your services.

It is simply all about them!

"Them" are your existing clients and future clients. These are the people who pay your bills and everything in this book is geared towards them.

This concept is a far cry from many existing marketing programs. Too many consultants start to sell their professional services before they have any inkling as to what the needs of their future clients are. They are too focused on themselves.

They are far too eager to sell themselves to their future clients and end up not understanding what the clients really want. Many consultants make this common mistake.

All you need to do is focus on defining and understanding your clients' needs and making connection with them.

Everything else will follow.

Chapter 1: What Really Goes on Inside the "New" Corporation

There has been a sea change in Corporate America resulting from downsizing. Many corporate departments have been downsized to a few individuals. For example, in many corporations, the environmental divisions have often been cut down to a few persons. Some engineering departments have all but disappeared. Many have been outsourced. All is left is a skeleton crew to select and manage consultants and contractors.

In the 1970s, corporations made purchasing decisions by committees. There was a reason for that. It was designed to provide collective coverage for the individual managers. It was designed to minimize individual accountability. Downsizing in the 1980s has changed all that. For example, the corporate environmental manager is often the sole decision-maker. His action is much more visible within the corporation and the "committee shield" is no longer there. He is more accountable than ever for his decision.

For consultants and other professionals alike, technical competence is now a necessary but not sufficient condition in getting the job. It now requires more than technical skills and competence to win a consulting assignment.

Several principals of large consulting firms made the following observations in an article published in the American Consulting Engineer Magazine:

"Consulting firms can no longer count on winning and keeping good clients solely on the basis of their technical capabiltiy or just the quality of their work. We find ourselves dealing less with engineers and more with chief financial officers."Such is the new paradigm in the real world.

With headcount reduction and restructuring, managers who work in these corporations are under an incredible amount of stress. Performance of senior management is gauged on a very short time frame. If the company is publicly traded, the demand for short-term performance is even more severe. It has to produce improved profits on a quarterly basis in order to satisfy the insatiable demands of Wall Street.

Internally, most managers have to show performance on a weekly or monthly basis. When a problem arises, these managers look for workable solutions in as short a time frame as possible. They look for professionals to fix their problem in a timely manner and/or save them money. Gone are the good old days when a consultant can come in, do an extensive study and get away with recommending further studies.

Corporations demand quick and cost-effective solutions.

For example, as a result of downsizing, many environmental managers have been assigned additional responsibilities such as safety, security and even sanitation. The time pressure on these individuals is intense. Many of them do not even have a support staff. And the manager is the committee in charge of buying professional services.

The adage that you can do more with less is never more true in Corporate America these days. You need to keep this in mind at all times when you sell your services to these companies. Corporate managers are looking for quick and cost-effective solutions to their problems.

How Do Companies Select Consultants?

In most instances, the process is done through "word of mouth" referral. If a consultant has done excellent work for one company, it is amazing how quickly words get around. The reverse is equally true. Bad consultants' reputation gets around just as quickly.

It is human nature that people are weary of hiring strangers. That's why referral is so important. People also like to work with people they like. And that's why interpersonal skill is paramount.

Another common means by which consultants are hired is based on past performance. That's right - repeat business. It has been estimated that over 80 percent of a successful Consultant's business come from repeat business. This is all the more reason why much of a consultant's marketing effort should be focused on satisfying his existing clients in order to reap the benefits of repeat business.

This concept is similar to that of a physician who is successful in treating a patient's ailment. Chances are very high that the recovered patient will come back to the same physician when he has another health problem. It is also very likely that the patient will also recommend this doctor to his friends and family.

That's repeat business - plain and simple.

Your future clients are always looking for the appropriate level of experience from their consultants to solve their problems. They are always very cautious in the selection process because the last thing they need is to hire the wrong consultant and create another internal corporate problem in addition to not having the original issues resolved. Keep in mind that when you ask your future clients to hire you, you are asking them to take a risk on you. To them, there is always the risk that you will not work out and that carries with it the stigma of failure on their part. Their colleagues and superiors within their organization will know about the failure.

In other words, clients want their consultants to make them look good within their organization. It is to your best interest to recognize this fact and interact with your clients accordingly. You must pay attention to their backgrounds, their hopes, their fears and their limitations within their own organizations.

You must pay close attention to your clients' internal "office politics". If there are detractors with the organization who may be against your clients, you need to be aware of it. This recognition must show through in your meetings, telephone conversations, emails and presentations. When your clients can sense that kind of respect from you, they will offer you the same respect. When they sense arrogance on your part, they will find a way to terminate the relationship very quickly. That's just human nature.

Your future clients will be looking for practical and innovative ways that you can help them to fix their problems. They are not looking for you to study the problem and recommend "additional studies." That's the old ways of consulting - propose a phased approach and turn the consulting assignment into a life-long (seems that way to the clients) billable project. Fewer and fewer companies are buying into this approach.

Your future clients are not looking for hype either. They don't really care how great your company is or how great it looks on a multi-colored brochure. If they feel that you know what you are talking about and that you understand their problems, they will consider hiring you. Remember – they are looking for solutions to a problem so that they can move on to deal with other problems.

For this reason, it is absolutely imperative that you listen to your clients' needs first and try to understand their particular problems. Only after you have achieved this level of understanding can you hope to propose a practical solution to their problems.

Is Cost the Real Determining Factor?

In general, the answer is no.

Cost is generally not the determining factor in the selection of consultants although it is often the first item your future client would look at. One big exception is in the public sector. Government agencies are often required by law to select the lowest "qualified bidder". Most companies have purchasing policies that may also require their managers to hire the lowest qualified consultant. But that policy can often be circumvented.

One thing to keep in mind: If you provide a valuable service and you can justify your billing rates, by all means stick with them. But at the same time, you need to be flexible in your billing practice. If your clients prefer a specific billing schedule or format that is more convenient for them, change your to fit theirs. It is all about them. Do not insist that your clients change their accounting system to fit yours. It ought to be the other way around.

The worst thing that can happen to a consultant's reputation is to slash his billing rates in order to get the job. Some consultants do that because they are just trying to get a foot in the door with a reduced rate and then make up for it later through repeat business or change orders.

That is a self-defeating approach.

Chances are your future clients know that strategy too. They will hire the consultant for the reduced rate just once and then move on to other firms or they will turn you down out right. If a firm is too cheap to pay you what you are worth, what makes you think it will change its behavior in the future.

If you cannot justify your billing rates to your future clients, you don't deserve to win the job. If you have a valid basis for your rates and your clients are resisting that, you probably want to think twice about working for such a client.

The following example illustrates the point.

An environmental manager interviewed four large consulting firms for an ocean disposal environmental impact study. Two of them came in within 5% of each other in price. The third one was about 30% higher.

The manager pointed out this fact to the high bidder during the interview. He was looking for the underlying reasons for higher costs thinking that the consultants may have a better team, more experience, etc. Instead of providing the client with justifications for the higher quotes, the consultant immediately offered to match his competitors in price. This set off an alarm in the client's head right away. It signaled three possibilities:

The consultant had built in such a large profit margin in the proposal that he was able to reduce his price by 30% and still be able to make a profit. The consultant was so desperate to get the job that he was willing to forego his profit or even take a loss. The consultant was just trying to get his foot in the door and then make up for the 30% reduction through future change orders.

None of these possibilities was attractive to the client and the consultant never got the job.

Many clients are astute and savvy enough to recognize the value associated with a consultant's rates. Very often they are willing to pay more as long as they think they will get better value for the higher rate. If they sense that a consultant understands their problems and has the capability to help them, they will often work with the consultant to make sure that he turns a decent profit. The clients will look for a win-win situation in this case.

Cost is usually not the sole determining factor in selecting a consultant. Many companies will not automatically go to the lowest bidder for consulting services.

Who Are the Real Buyers?

So who are the real decision-makers? Who are the ones who make the final decision to hire you?

In the 70s and early 80s, the buyers were made up of individuals who were members of committees. It was designed to provide "coverage" for the individual managers since it was always a committee that made the purchasing decision collectively. If the wrong buying decision was made, it was the committee that made it and there was little individual accountability or culpability.

This is no longer the case.

Downsizing of big businesses has resulted in lean staffs within the corporate structure. Decisions - including purchasing decisions - are increasingly being made on an individual basis and not by committees. The reality is that very few companies have purchasing committees! Organizations that still have selection committees are government agencies and trade associations.

Chapter 7 discusses some nuances you need to know when going before a selection committee.

Your clients are looking for quick and cost-effective solutions. They are already overloaded with work. What they want their consultants to do is to come in, do the job, and get out.

The real buyers of professional services are corporate managers, plant managers and operations and production managers. These are the "end users". They are over worked and understaffed. They are the ones who will be most directly affected by the choice of consultants or consultants.

In most instances the real buyers are not the purchase agents from the purchasing department. These people are administrators of paperwork. They merely churn out the purchase orders after the decision has been made by the real decision-maker - the end user.

Senior executives are too busy planning the next downsizing scheme to get involved in deciding which consultants to hire. That task is delegated (by default) to managerial levels. The role of legal counsel in hiring professional help (other than outsourcing legal work) is very limited except in cases involving environmental due diligence as part of corporate acquisition or projects that carry significant environmental liability.

Corporate attorneys may also be involved in hiring consultants to do independent environmental audits in order to secure attorney-client privilege.

Chapter 2: How to Approach Your Future Clients

Corporations are looking for quick and cost-effective solutions. What they want consultants to do is to come in, identify the problems, fix them, and get out.

When you are selling services, you must sell from the standpoint of the buyer. The bottom line is this - the buyer will buy only if he has something to gain from his purchasing decision.

Is his decision going to make him look good in the eyes of his supervisor?

Is the buyer looking for something to shake things up within the corporation?

All of these internal personnel matters play a role in the decision making process. When you are selling your professional services, you must sell from the viewpoint of your future client.

As stated earlier, your future client will only buy your services if he has something to gain from his purchasing decision. Is his buying decision going to make him look good in the eyes of his supervisor? Will you be able to fix his problems for him - in a timely and cost-effective manner? Will you make him a corporate "hero" if he hires you?

He is looking to you the consultant to provide him with coverage. His hiring decision – if it is the correct one – should make him look good. In other words, what's good for your client is good for you.

The Issue of Prices

This is often a very tricky issue with many consultants. Just when is the best time to bring up your hourly rates and what to do when this subject comes up with your future clients?

There are two types of clients. The first type looks for value in consultants. They see consultants as outside experts who can bring a fresh perspective and approach to solving their problems. These clients don't mind paying more as long as they are convinced that the consultants are worth the money.

The second type of clients looks for consultants with the lowest rate. They don't understand or much care about value. These are the clients that would hire "Bob the midnight hauler" to ship their hazardous wastes simply because Bob is the lowest bidder. These are also the ones who shop for the cheapest brain surgeon in town when they have a brain tumor. Stay away from these clients. They will nickel and dime you to death after you get the job. Why would you want to do business with them?

Never discount your fees for the sole purpose of getting the job. It cheapens your services. Don't tell your future clients you will match your competitor's fees. It sends a message that you will do anything to get the job and that maybe you are desperate for work.

The following is taken from a book called "Frogs into Princes" by Steve Andres.

There is an old story of a boilermaker who was hired to fix a huge steamship boiler system that was not working well. After listening to the engineer's description of the problems and asking a few questions, he went to the boiler room. He looked at the maze of twisting pipes, listened to the thump of the boiler and the hiss of escaping steam for a few minutes, and felt some pipes with his hands. Then he hummed softly to himself, reached into his overalls and took out a small hammer, and tapped a bright red valve, once. Immediately, the entire system began working perfectly, and the boilermaker went home. When the steamship owner received a bill for $1,000 he complained that the boilermaker had only been in the engine room for fifteen minutes, and requested an itemized bill. This is what the boilermaker sent him:

> For tapping with a hammer: 50 cents.
> For knowing where to tap: $999.50
> Total: $1000.00

The fees you charge your client should be in direct proportion to the true value of your expertise.

Here is another story to illustrate the point:

An extremely wealthy man was convicted of murder and sentenced to death. He spent millions of dollars on a team of legal experts to get him out of death row. After years of court challenges and millions of dollars of legal fees, his case was rejected by the Supreme Court. The only way he could be spared from execution now was a commutation by the governor. His high priced legal team tried to call the governor and was not able to get to him. He was to be executed the next day.

A high priced criminal defense attorney came to the inmate in death row and told him that he could help him because the attorney happened to be a very close personal friend of the governor's. The attorney picked up the phone in the death row and called his friend the governor at his official residence. In 15 minutes of conversation, the attorney was able to convince the governor to commute the death sentence to a life sentence.

The question is this: How much should the millionaire convict pay the attorney who saved his life? Should he pay $100 for 15 minutes of the attorney's time or should he pay a little bit more?

A good client looks for cost-effective solutions from his consultants. He is not necessarily looking for the lowest cost solution. In fact, if your offer price is too low, your client will often get suspicious. They don't want to deal with a consultant who is low-balling the project just to "get in the door". They don't want to have to deal with change orders later.

When you discuss fees with your future clients, always keep in mind that they may have specific preference on how the fee structure should be set up. For example, not all of your clients want to pay you by the hour on a time and material basis. Some may prefer that you quote them a lump sum for performing the entire task. Others may want to put you on a retainer basis.

Whatever your future clients desire, you need to accede to their preference. Always remember that you work for them – and not the other way around.

Modify your internal billing method to suit theirs. They are your customers. You work for them. For example, some clients may not want you to itemize all your incidental expenses on your invoices because they don't want to have to justify them internally within their own bureaucracy. If that is the case, modify your invoices in accordance with your client's request. Don't ever tell your clients that you can't because your accounts receivable people refuse to change their standard invoice format.

What Should You Emphasize In Your Sales Pitch

We all have the experience of walking into a clothing store or car dealership and are immediately stalked by some sales clerk who follows us around until we walk out in disgust. A good salesman, on the other hand, allows the customers to look around and get to know the merchandise. He is available for questions. This is the main reason car dealerships encourage you to test drive the car that you want. A good salesman will not pepper you with questions. He will just ask you if you like the car and if you would like to take it out for a spin. He is hoping that you will like the new car so much that you will convince yourself that you really deserve it even though it may be out of your price range.

What he is doing is letting the customers sell themselves.

You should do the same as a consultant. Let your future client determine by himself that you are qualified for the job and your fees will not be much of a problem. It is common for the client to go out of his way to promote a new consultant simply because he is convinced that this is the right one for the company. A client would recommend a good consultant to others within his organization if he is convinced that the great work of that consultant would enhance his own reputation. So it is to your client's own best interest to hire the right consultant.

In their eagerness to get a new consulting contract, many consultants fall into the trap of spending way too much time talking about themselves at the first meeting with their future clients - often to their own detriment.

Remember this: Marketing gets you in front of the client and nothing more. It is selling that will get you the job.

Before a consultant has the slightest chance of landing a job, he must first understand the potential client's problem.

A case in point, how can a doctor diagnose an ailment without understanding what ails the patient? The trick of the trade is a six-letter word: **L-I-S-T-E-N**. The doctor does that by asking a lot of questions and listening to the answers. An effective and successful consultant does the same thing. He always listens to his client's problems first. He listens before he talks. A smart consultant focuses on the client's needs – instead of bragging about how great he is or how wonderful his consulting firm is.

The successful consultant asks a lot of questions and then he listens to the answers. He analyzes his client's problems carefully. And then he comes up with a cost-effective solution. After all, that's what the client wants first and foremost - a cost-effective solution.

The stereotypical image of a super salesman as a slick smooth talker is a relic of the past. That's a snake oil salesman. In fact, surveys after surveys have demonstrated that the top sales people are the ones who are – first and foremost - good listeners. They let their customers talk 60 to 70 percent of the time. They wait to offer solutions or products to the customers only after they have listened and understood their customer's needs and concerns.

The client always wants to know how long it will take the consultant to fix the problem since the client is accountable to his senior management for getting the problem fixed in a timely and cost-effective manner.

The trick is to be able to sit down in front of the client, ask a couple of open ended questions, then shut up and listen to the answers. That's the only way to understand your future client's problems.

Always Focus on Your Strength and Project the Right Image

If you are an owner-operated business, the best strategy is to emphasize this fact and use it to your advantage. You need to differentiate your company from your competitors.

To compete against the large firms, your strategy is to turn their perceived strength (size) into a weakness.

Your sales pitch would be that as the owner of your business, you have a vested personal interest in ensuring your clients get the best service possible. Therefore you as the owner-consultant will check up on your staff to make sure that the service is of the highest quality. Let your clients know that not just by telling them – but by doing it. Call up your clients on a regular basis and ask them about how satisfied they are with your staff's work. Give them your personal phone number so that they can get hold of you when there is a problem. That's your strength. That's what sets you apart from those giant consulting firms. Your client will understand and appreciate your thoughtfulness.

The key to marketing is to emphasize your particular strength that is relevant to the client's problem. The key word here is "relevant". There is no point in telling your client something that has no meaning to her. If you are a small family-owned consulting firm, your strength lies in the fact that it is your business and you take personal pride and responsibility on everything your staff does for the clients. Emphasize that your firm is your business. Tell your client that you are available to her 24/7 and that if she is not happy with your staff's performance, you will take personal responsibility and see to it that the problem gets resolved.

Give your clients your home phone number. Tell them to call you any time they have a problem with your job. Chances are they won't call you but they will appreciate and remember the gesture.

You want to play to your strength (small, nimble, responsive with personal accountability) and contrast it with your competitors' weakness (large, less responsive and more bureaucratic.) Such comparison separates you from your competitors.

Unfortunately, not all owner-operated consulting firms heed this advice.

The following real life example demonstrates it:

The owner of a small consultant firm based in New Mexico wanted to get feedback from his small list of clients. So he established a policy of surveying his clients on the quality of work performed by his engineering staff.

Every quarter, he mailed out survey letters to his clients on letterheads that read "Office of the Chairman and Chief Executive Officer" and had his Director of Business Development sign the letters.

He was trying to present himself as the head of a conglomerate like IBM. He ended up losing his best advantage - the personal touch and responsiveness of a lean and mean entrepreneurial organization. The survey letter looked pretentious and pompous – coming from a small firm like his.

It is quite ironic that many big corporations these days are trying to be nimble and responsive and yet this tiny boutique consulting firm was pretending to be a behemoth and dinosaur all at the same time!

If you work in a large consulting firm, you want to project your image very carefully. For example, if your future client has a leaking underground storage tank in Idaho, would he be impressed by the fact that your firm has 95 offices in 30 countries on 5 continents? What does this bit of information mean to a corporate environmental manager who has a localized problem that needs to be addressed quickly? The prudent marketing approach in this case would be to tell your future client that you would assign a more junior but experienced engineer to this project at a reasonable hourly rate. Focus on convincing your future client that he will get the results that he desires rather than on the size and reach of your firm. The fact that you have offices throughout the world is totally irrelevant to him.

On the other hand, if you were bidding on a job to perform worldwide environmental audits for a multi-national conglomerate, you would of course emphasize the global reaches of your operation - provided your 95 offices are not too far from your future clients' facilities. Your selling point to the client would be on the fact that you could save him a substantial amount of travel costs by having consultants close to the places where he needs auditing done.

The Uniquely Qualified and Full Service Firms

One of the mistakes often made by consultants is that they believe that they can be all things to all people. An even worst mistake is to actually tell their future clients that they are all things to all people. It seems that any firm with more than 10 persons is now billed as a full-service firm that somehow possesses the unique qualification to do whatever its clients want.

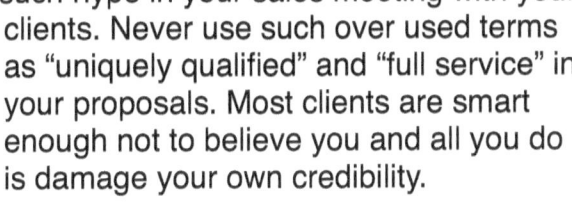

Avoid using such hype in your sales meeting with your clients. Never use such over used terms as "uniquely qualified" and "full service" in your proposals. Most clients are smart enough not to believe you and all you do is damage your own credibility.

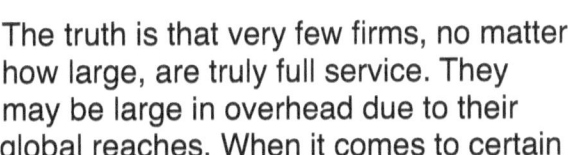

The truth is that very few firms, no matter how large, are truly full service. They may be large in overhead due to their global reaches. When it comes to certain tasks, they often subcontract out their work and mark up the fees to their clients. Your future clients know that too.

More and more corporations are reluctant to retain this type of "full service" consulting firms. Many companies would rather approach experienced and responsive small specialty firms that can perform the special task without the added costs of administrative fees and mark-ups.

Selling Your Services - the Basics

The first thing you need to do is to seek out the real decision-makers - the ones who tell the Purchasing Department to put your name on the purchase order. Depending on the complexity and cost of the job these decision-makers can be a vice president, a senior manager or a supervisor.

And how do you find out who these people are?

The answer is very simple: By asking the right questions of your clients, listening more to the answers and talking much less about yourself.

It is a known fact that **people like to do business with people they like**. The process by which corporate managers select consultants is no different. Once you develop a personal rapport with your future clients, they will listen to you.

You should always hire people who like other people. This is a people business. Promote your staff members who know how to get along with your clients. Knowledge is important but without inter-personal skills, a consultant's career is limited.

The best time of day to sell your service is to get your future client to have lunch with you. You want to get him out of his office - away from his daily distractions – so that you can listen to him talk. The idea is to listen to your client – and not have your client listen to you.

It was Abraham Lincoln who said that people don't care how much you know until they know how much you care. This is a very wise saying.

You need to let your clients know that you really care about helping them to fix their problems. The best way to demonstrate that is by listening to their problems.

When you are listening to your client, try to take notes as well. By taking notes, you are showing your client that you think she is smart and you take what she says to you seriously. After you have listed to her problems, you should make an attempt to summarize what you have just heard to make sure there is no misunderstanding on your part. It shows your client that you are serious and you are conscientious

Your future clients could care less about your past history as long as they feel comfortable that you can do the job for them. They could care less about how great you are, how great your company is, how many offices you have, how many PhDs per square foot, etc. One consulting firm actually stated the number of PhDs per square foot in its brochure. Your clients want one thing and one thing only from you. They want you to fix their problems. They are looking for the individual who can solve their problems for them. The name of your company matters a lot less to your future clients than the person assigned to do the job.

They generally choose the person and not the firm. And if you do not have rapport with that client, he will not hire you no matter how great your firm is.

In reality, you are not trying to convince your clients to buy your services. You are in fact trying to give your future clients reasons to select you. It is a proven fact that people buy for emotional reasons and justify the decision later intellectually.

After you have had your luncheon with your future client, make sure you ask for referrals. If the client has no need for your services at this time, he may know someone who does. It never hurts to ask for referrals. This is of course equally true if you are dealing with an existing client. Make your next sell by following up on your work.

Chapter 3: Listening to Your Future Clients

"One of the best ways to persuade others is with your ears – by listening to them."

– Dean Rusk – former U.S. Secretary of State.

Successful sales professionals in all walks of life have one thing in common: They are all very good listeners. They listen to their potential customers.

They usually spend at least two-thirds of their time listening to their clients' needs by asking open ended questions and the remaining time answering questions or clarifying situation. Listening is the most effective way of identifying sales opportunities.

You have to understand your client's requirement before you can help him.

The Art of Active Listening

What is active listening?

This is a technique used by many seasoned and successful sales professionals. They listen to their customers first and summarize what they have heard. This approach gives the client a chance to correct any misunderstanding or misconception. It also reinforces the idea that they are listening and paying attention to the client's needs. Nothing irritates a client more than being ignored by his consultant. Active listening is also helpful when a client raises an objection to either the cost or technical approach. By engaging in a dialog early, you are positioning yourself to eliminate these objections as they arise.

Always listen to the client's problems. If you are talking, you are not listening.

In his book "The Professional Service Firm 50", Tom Peters talks about the 2:1 ear to mouth ratio. You have two ears and one mouth. You should spend at least twice as much time using your ears than your mouth. He also tells owners of professional firms to pay special attention to those few employees who are quiet. These are the ones with big ears. They are often the ones who listen to their future clients' problems and come up with exceptional insights on how to solve those problems. Their ears and brains are often engaged – but not their mouths.

Ask yourself these questions:

1. Do you interrupt your client before she is finished talking? Never do that! It is rude and it also tells your client you are not really interested in what she has to say.

2. Do you listen for "hot buttons" that excite your client? You should watch for these hot button topics and try to establish rapport with your client by engaging in conversation with her.

3. Are you paying close attention when your client is talking? Look your client right in the eyes to show your commitment to listening. Take notes to show her you are serious about helping her.

4. Are you giving your client signals that you are actually listening to her? You should make listening noises such as "oh", "really", "I see" to reassure your client that you are following her.

Do you talk too much at your meetings with future clients? Here is a story that illustrates the peril of talking a little too much.

During the French revolution three prominent, but very unfortunate, professionals were condemned to

beheading by the guillotine: a priest, a doctor, and an engineer. The three were conveyed to the scaffold together in an old ox cart and were marched up to the guillotine together amidst a mass of cheering blood thirsty spectators.

The priest was the first to meet his fate. The executioner very politely asked the priest if he preferred to avoid seeing the blade fall by lying face down rather than face up. The priest replied, "I've led a good life, have nothing to regret, and want to meet my maker face-to-face." So the priest lied down facing the blade. The executioner pulled the cord releasing the blade and it plummeted toward the priest's exposed neck. But within a half inch of reaching its fatal destination the blade stopped literally in its tracks. The crowd roared with delight and many of the onlookers fell to their knees in prayer. Not wanting to put any victim to double jeopardy the authorities released the priest, to the great delight of the crowd.

Then came the doctor's turn. He was asked the same question and thought "if it worked for the priest maybe it will work for me too," so he requested to take the blade face up. Again the blade stopped a half inch from the target, and as with the priest, the authorities released the doctor.

Now was the engineer's turn and, being no one's fool, he also opted to take the blade face up. As he lay with his neck firmly placed in the crook of the guillotine and looked up to his maker, and to the blade, he exclaimed, "Ooh, I think I see your problem."

Sometimes - less is better.

Always Look for High Quality Information

Our present day perception of the world is very much shaped by our past. What we have experienced in our past defines who we are and how we see the world around us. It provides us with a road map to the future. In other words, our view of the world is often shaped by what we experienced in the past. It is extremely likely that you and your future clients share totally different past experiences and therefore have completely different road maps and views of the world. The following illustrates this point:

A Harvard Business School professor divided his class into two groups. He gave the two groups two different drawings and asked each group to look at its own set of drawing intensely for 30 seconds.

These were the two drawings.

The first group was shown this drawing on the left. The second group was shown the drawing on the right.

Neither group was allowed to look at the other's drawing.

The professor then showed the entire class a third drawing on the left and asked each group to describe it.

The first group was adamant that it showed a young lady wearing a necklace with her face turned sideways. The second group of students said the third drawing was an old woman with a hooked nose and scarf over her head. The two groups got into a heated argument. Each was equally sure that the other group was wrong and quite possibly insane.

It was not until the professor asked each group to show the other group exactly where the necklace and hooked nose were located that the students began to understand the other side's perspective.

Both groups of students were equally correct in their perception of the third drawing. The way each group viewed the third drawing was very much influenced by its exposure the other drawings earlier. Because they had different experiences in the past, they came to two diametrically opposite views of the world. The argument was resolved only after each side explained its own past experience and was made aware of the other side's.

The resolution came only after each side was given higher quality information. This experiment also demonstrate the dramatic impact of first impression. Whatever you see first will shade your perception for a long time.

The trick for you as a consultant is to share your road map with your client so that you are both on the same journey – at least for the duration of your project.

Miscommunication and misunderstanding develop when people use different standards of measurement to define performance. For example, the salesman measures his own job performance by the number of sales orders he has taken. His boss – the general manager – bases his own performance on the amount of revenue coming into the company at any given time. So if the cash is slow coming into the company's bank account, the general manager may accuse the salesman of not selling enough goods while the salesman feels that he is not being appreciated for his hard work. Miscommunication leads to conflict in this case.

This conflict can very easily be averted if the participants involved look for better quality information. They would have discovered that the problem lies with the billing clerk who has been very tardy in mailing out invoices.

Consider the following examples of low and higher quality information:

Low Quality Information	Higher Quality Information
Let's meet next week in downtown Los Angeles.	Let's meet at 3:00 pm next Wednesday at the coffee shop on 123 Main Street in downtown Los Angeles.
We have numerous violations of our wastewater discharge permit.	We violated 4 parameters (TSS, pH, temperature and chlorine) 7 times last month.
The groundwater was contaminated.	The aquifer was contaminated with TCE with an average concentration of 200 ppm and the contamination plume was heading towards the American River.

As a consultant, which type of information would you like to have from your client?

One way to judge whether you have high quality information is to apply the wheelbarrow test. If you can put the bit of information in a mental wheelbarrow, it is more likely than not to be of high quality.

For example, if your client tells you that he wants you to install 50 red telephones in his offices, that is high quality information. You can put the red telephones in a wheelbarrow. You know exactly what he means. But if he tells you he wants you to improve his inter-office communication system, that's low quality information. You cannot place "inter-office communication system" in your mental wheelbarrow. You will want to ask him more questions to find out what exactly he wants from you.

In their fabulous linguistic book "The Structure of Magic", Richard Bandler and John Grinder give more examples of words that can and cannot be placed in a mental wheelbarrow:

These cannot be put in a wheelbarrow	These can be put in a wheelbarrow
I have a lot of frustration	I have lots of green marble
I expect help	I expect a letter

These cannot be put in a wheelbarrow	These can be put in a wheelbarrow
My fear is too great	My coat is too big
I lost my temper	I lost my book
I need love	I need a bottle of water
Failure frightens me	Horses frighten me
The tension bothers me	The dragon bothers me

Which type of information would you like to have at a meeting with your client?

At your meetings with your future clients, always look for high quality information. This is part of the active listening process - a process by which you look for information that is both specific and precise.

Another reason for obtaining high quality information is that it will help you avoid making the wrong assumptions about a situation or a person.

To obtain high quality information, you need to ask open ended questions.

The level of quality of information you should seek is determined by your desired outcome. It is like looking at an aerial photograph of a large facility. If you are only interested in determining the outer boundary of a site, you probably don't need to zoom in too much on the aerial photograph. But if you are trying to see how many drums of chemicals are being kept outside in the backyard of a factory, you would want to zoom in much deeper and get a much higher resolution of the aerial photo.

Here is a very good example of how to obtain higher quality information from your future clients in a meeting:

Client: Thanks for coming. I have a real big problem.

Consultant: Oh…specifically what kind of problems are you having?

Client: We have problems with our hazardous waste disposal practice.

Consultant: What was the problem with your hazardous waste disposal practice?

Client: I got called into the General Manager's office and got chewed out by my boss. He was very upset.

Consultant: Sorry to hear that. What was he upset about?

Client: His office just received a Notice of Violation from the county.

Consultant: What was the nature of the violation?

Client: Well – apparently the county inspector was at one of our plants last month and he did a dumpster dive.

Consultant: A dumpster dive? What was he looking for?

Client:	He found a number of half empty aerosol spray cans in the dumpster.
Consultant	Hmmm…..I think I know where this is heading. What specifically was the nature of the citation?
Client:	Illegal disposal of hazardous waste. He found a number of spray cans that were still pressurized and therefore considered to be reactive.
Consultant:	Yes…that's true. Any waste that is reactive must be disposed of as hazardous waste. You half empty spray cans are reactive. How many spray cans does your company throw out a day?
Client:	I would think about 30 cans per location per day.
Consultant:	How many locations do you have?
Client:	A total of six locations.
Consultant:	How many of these cans do you estimate are truly empty – I mean – not pressurized?
Client:	Gee…I have no way of knowing short of testing every spray can that is being tossed out.

So let's see what the consultant found out from this series of questions. The meeting started out with the client saying he had a "real big problem". That statement is of the lowest quality. It did not give the consultant any information to work with. A "real big problem" could mean many different things to many people.

By asking the right questions, the consultant was able to determine that his client's organization threw out about 180 aerosol spray cans a day and that some of them were empty and others were not. The consultant also knew that the county inspector would make a point of jumping into the dumpster to look for the pressurized cans.

So now the consultant has sufficient high quality information on which to formulate recommendations to this client. There are several options available to the client in this case. One – he can assign someone the specific responsibility of checking out every single one of the 180 empty cans a day and separate out those that are still pressurized and dispose of them as reactive hazardous waste. Two – he can make a management decision to dispose of all spray cans as hazardous waste regarding of the residual pressure in them. Or the third option would be to train his employees to properly identify each can prior to disposal and place it in either two separate bins – one for pressurized cans and the other for non-pressurized cans.

All of these three options have advantages and draw backs. But they would all achieve the desired outcome of complying with waste disposal regulations and avoiding being cited by the county.

Asking Open-ended Questions

When you are listening to your future clients, you should be on the lookout for terms such as: "we can't", "we have to", "it is impossible", "we must", "that's out of the question", "no way can we do that", "it is absolutely essential". These phrases limit your future client's choices and options. They place restrictions on what the client thinks he can or cannot do. Your job as an effective consultant is to open up more choices for your client by posing open-ended questions such as:

      What would happen if you _____?
      What stops you from _____?
      How specifically can you _____?
      Who is responsible for _____?
      When do you do this _____?

    These types of questions force the client to think about his situation and open up other possibilities for him that he might now have ever considered before. The self-imposed restrictions of your client may well turn out to be valid after you have asked the right questions. That's fine. At least now you know for sure. But often than not, you will find that these open-ended questions actually open up a new host of possibilities for your client. He may not have thought about other possibilities simply because his company has always done certain things in a certain way. How often have you heard someone say this: "Oh…I don't know. We have always done it this way." This is particularly true in large corporations.

    Challenge your client's assumptions – in a nice way of course. If you hear any definitive or all-inclusive types of declaration from your client, ask probing questions.

Client's statement	Your question
All of the machines need fixing	All of them? Specifically which ones need fixing?
The whole plant is not working	Which specific parts of the plant are not working?
My operating costs are way up	Which costs in particular are going up?

Very often, when people think something cannot be done, it is because they think or assume that it is too costly. Or because they feel that it has always been done that way, so there is no reason to change. In general, people avoid risk or change because they do not have high quality information. It is much easier to fall back to the position that "it worked before, why change it now?"

By asking your client some probing questions, you may help him to look at the cost/benefit aspect of the problem with a different angle and end up helping him to redefine his cost.

A very effective way to help your future client or you break through this mental block is by asking "what if" questions.

When you are asking "what if" questions, you are penetrating the "off limits" and "out of bound" areas and challenging your clients to look at other possibilities and choices. This is a common method used by psychologists and therapists. By opening up the world for your future clients, you are doing them and yourself a favor. The end result will be a much more cost-effective solution for the client and possibly a new assignment for you --- your ultimate objective.

Here are a few examples of "what if" questions:

Client's comments	Your Questions
We can't change that purchasing policy	What would happen if you did?
We can't change that purchasing policy	What if you give them a better alternative?

Consider the following exchange between a future client and his consultant about awarding a contract:

Client: Thank you for taking the time to meet with me on such short notice.

Consultant: We are glad to be here to help you in any way.

Client: I really like your proposal. It has some very good ideas that none of your competitors came up with.

Consultant I am glad you like our ideas. We put a lot of thoughts into our proposal.

Client: Yes…I know. It really shows. But we have a big problem here. Your price is not the least expensive one. And we have a company policy that says I am supposed to go with

43

	the qualified consultant with the lowest price.
Consultant	Oh….I am sorry to hear that. Are the consultants with the lowest cost qualified?
Client:	Yes I am afraid they are. But you know - I really don't like them. I am not too fond of their approach. And I don't care much for their project manager either. He seems kind of arrogant and aloof. There is not much chemistry between us. I would rather go with you guys. I think you guys would do a great job for us. But we have this policy that we have to go with the lowest bidder.
Consultant:	I understand and I appreciate your vote of confidence in us. You are in a bit of a situation here. Let me ask you this: what would happen if you were to go against that company policy?
Client:	Those guys in the Purchasing Department would raise hell and probably refuse to write up the Purchase Order.
Consultant:	We sure don't want that to happen.
Client:	No we don't.
Consultant:	What would your boss's reaction be if he were to find out that you were going against the company policy?
Client:	I don't think he would be very happy either.

Consultant	Now what if you were to give him a one-page memo outlining the fact that you would be getting a bigger bang for the dollar if you were to select us? Would he consider that?
Client:	Yes…I think so.
Consultant:	Would senior management consider that too?
Client:	Sure…they are all very focused on the bottom-line.
Consultant:	Great! Let us prepare a one-page cost justification for you to give to your boss. Maybe he can go to bat for you.
Client:	If the bottom-line supports it, he will back up. He has done that a number of times before.
Consultant:	What's going to happen to those guys in the Purchasing Department?
Client:	If the numbers look good, someone higher up will over-rule that policy. Our Chief Financial Officer is a pretty sharp business woman. She will recognize a good deal when she sees one.
Consultant:	Wonderful. We will also show in the memo that by choosing us, your department will help your company significantly reduce its long term environmental liability as well.

	What if your legal department were to come across that memo?
Client:	That's a great idea. The attorneys would love that. And my boss would really like that because that would make him look good with those attorneys.
Consultant	Great….we will get busy on that memo for you right away.
Client:	Thank you. I look forward to working with you.

This is a classic case of the consultant helping his future client overcome an internal obstacle with a positive outcome for all.

By asking some simple "what if" questions, the consultant is able to help his client find a way around his company policy and end up making everyone (except for the purchasing guys) look good.

Asking the Right Questions

To get a better sense of your future client's needs, you need to ask the "right" questions. These are open-ended questions.

It is often better not to ask questions that start with "Why ….?" Because such questions generally result in defensive answers from your future clients. The questions represent a demand for justification. You don't' want to do that because that may put your client in an awkward situation. It is much better to ask the "how", "what", "who", "when" and "what if" types of open ended questions.

Consider another exchange between the consultant and the future client:

Client: Thank you for coming. The reason I asked you here is to see if you can solve my problem.

Consultant: What specific problem are you having now?

Client: My treatment plant operators are not meeting the discharge limits and I think raining is needed.

Consultant: Oh…I am sorry to hear that. Tell me, which specific limits are not being met?

Client: We have had to file violations on at least 7 parameters.

Consultant Which ones specifically?

Client:	Let me see....there is pH, suspended solids, oil and grease, cadmium, BOD, coliforms, and temperature.
Consultant:	I see... and how often have you had these violations?
Client:	This has been going on for some time now.
Consultant:	Specifically how many times?
Client:	I think six times in the last year.
Consultant:	OK...now about the training....what kind of training are your operators getting now?
Client:	They are not getting any training right now.
Consultant:	When was the last time someone got any training at all?
Client:	I think it was 2 years ago...yes...two years ago last month.
Consultant:	How many got trained......do you remember?
Client:	Two of them, I believe.
Consultant:	What type of training did they get?
Client:	Basic treatment plant operation.
Consultant:	How many people work at the plant?
Client:	There are six including the secretary.

Consultant: How many do you think need training in plant operation?

Client: I think all of them need training, except for the secretary.

Consultant: All of them?

Client: Yes..I think so.

Consultant: All of them…including the chemist?

Client: Hmmm…let me think…maybe not the chemist

Consultant: Yes....maybe the chemist needs different types of training…like chemical analytical procedures.

Client: Yes…I think you are right.

Consultant: When was the last time the chemist got any training?

Client: I am not sure he ever got any.

Consultant: That's interesting. Maybe we should look at his log book and see if he has been following the proper procedures for sample collection and analysis.

Client: That's a good idea.

Consultant: What if some of your "violations" really came from analytical errors and not operational error?

Client: I hadn't thought about that!

Consultant: Well…let me review the log book and give you some recommendations on specific training needs for your staff.

Client: Thank you.

All of these simple open-ended questions are designed to bring in much higher quality information for you to take back to your office. Remember that you are trying to diagnose your client's problem for him and convince him that you are the one who can solve his problem for him.

Never assume that your potential client understands his own problem. Your job at this stage is to help him diagnose his own problem and identify a cost effective solution. You can only do that if you have high quality information. With such high quality information, you can then come up with a cost-effective training program that will address your future client's concerns at a reasonable cost and land you the job.

Unfortunately, many other consultants, when faced with the above business opportunity, would jump at the chance and say; "Sure, we do a lot of training. We have many PEs and Ph.D.s in our office. I can send a team over next week and start your training." This is before they have any idea as to the true need of their clients. The end result is inevitably an overly expensive job that will keep them from getting any future business. It is a very shortsighted and self-defeating approach.

Here is another example: If your sales person comes to you and tells you that "sales increased last year and that it was a good year", he has not conveyed to you any high quality information at all. All you know is that sales were better last year and you have no idea what he means by "a good year". On the other hand, if someone were to tell you that you made $2 million more profit last year than the year before, you can gauge that performance and decide for yourself if it was indeed a good year or not. That's high quality information.

At the end of your meeting with your future client, you should always try to summarize your understanding of his problem and make sure he agrees with you. You want to start the project off with both of you using the same road map.

There is an excellent book on the subject of how to get high quality information in the business world. It is entitled "Precision – A New Approach to Communication" by Michael McMaster and John Grinder. It gives you many specific case studies of how good business managers ask the right questions to get high quality information.

Alway remember that words are just symbols. They do not represent reality. Different cultures use different symbols to communicate within themselves. Symbols are often ambiguous and subject to different interpretations even within the same culture depending on the life experience of the listeners.

Consider the following case study with two very different outcomes:

A Meeting With Bad Outcome

Below is a rather common exchange between a consultant and his future client.

Client: Thank you for coming. I really appreciate your coming here on such short notice.

Consultant: We are glad to be here.

Client: The reason I am having this meeting is because I think I am having big problems with our environmental compliance program at one of our manufacturing plants.

Consultant I am sorry to hear that. I am sure we can help you with that. We have 3000 consultants spread out in 48 locations throughout the country. We are one of largest consulting firms in the world. We are a full service consulting firm and we are uniquely qualified to ….

Client: Excuse me. Don't you want to know what problems I am having?

Consultant: Sorry. What are the problems?

Client: We have been having a lot of problems meeting our wastewater discharge permit limits.

Consultant   Wastewater treatment plant? That's our specialty! We can help you there. We have 14 consultants with PhDs in sanitary engineering. Let me show you our brochures and Statement of Qualifications.

Client: Maybe later......Let me get back with you on this. Thank you for coming.

A Meeting With Good Outcome

A much more productive exchange could have taken place as shown below:

Client: Thank you for coming. I really appreciate your coming here on such short notice.

Consultant: We are glad to be here to see what we can do for you.

Client: The reason I am having this meeting is because I think I am having big problems with our environmental compliance program at one of our manufacturing plants.

Consultant   I am sorry to hear that. What problems are you having at the plant specifically?

Client: The plant seems to be having a lot of problems meeting its wastewater discharge permit limits.

Consultant: What limits are they having problems with?

Client: Well...mainly with their temperature limit.

53

Consultant	I see. Many of your competitors have similar problems with temperature limit too. Are there any other parameters your plant is having problems with?
Client:	Yes…they also have problems with BOD and suspended solids.
Consultant	How frequently are they having these violations?
Client:	Too often for my comfort. They had to report 5 violations in their discharge Monitoring Report last month and the month before that.
Consultant	Let me ask you about the temperature problem.
Client:	Sure. Go ahead.
Consultant	How many boilers do you have at that plant?
Client:	Oh…let me think. We have 6 boilers we use to generate steam for cooking our canned goods. Why do you ask?
Consultant: causes	At the same time when you have your temperature issue – you know – when the temperature goes outside of the permitted range – have you checked to see if your plant is discharging boiler blow down? That could quite possibly be a reason that the periodic temperature violation. I have

seen that happened a few times at other plants.

Client: Wow...I hadn't thought about that. I should look into it. Thanks for the tip. Let's talk about what more your firm can do for us. We can always use a few good consultants.

An Analysis of the two meetings

Let's see what happened at the bad meeting. The consultant never bothered to ask his future client about the "problems" he was having. He was too eager to sell his company. He was too eager to tell his future client what his firm could do without ever understanding his client's problem. This is like a doctor telling his patient how great he is before ever hearing what ails his patient. The consultant certainly did not give the client the feeling that he was there to help him with his problem. There was no empathy at all. The consultant gave his future client the distinct impression that he was there to sell a job and nothing else mattered. The meeting did not last very long.

Now let's take a look at what happened at the good meeting. The consultant never once mentioned how great his company was. He listened to the client's comment about "having big problems" at one of the plants. He showed empathy. He also jumped right in and asked specifically about the "problems". In a series of simple and direct questions, the consultant was able to find out the nature and frequency of the future client's problems. That's high quality information that he needed to start the process of helping his client. He then went on to diagnose the temperature problem based on his own professional experience.

In this relatively short exchange, the consultant was able to establish rapport with his future client, provide free advice, gain his confidence and secure a business relationship that would likely lead to new business.

That's what high quality information can get you.

The Doctor-Patient Model

The way companies hire consultants is very similar to the way people selected their personal physicians. You should view yourself as the medical doctor and your future client as your "patient".

Your future clients are always looking for competent professionals to fix their problems as quickly and as cheaply as possible.

When a patient comes through the door, one of the first things a doctor does is to listen to what ails his patient. He listens to how the patient describes the symptoms, how it hurts, where it hurts, etc. He asks probing questions. He probes. He goes through the process of eliciting high quality information to determine what is really causing discomfort to his patient. The doctor then orders certain tests to confirm the accuracy of his diagnosis.

Only after he has done all that will the doctor prescribe the proper treatment to cure the sickness.

Why should a consultant be any different?

When you walk through the door to see your family physician, surely he does not tell you right away how great a doctor he is and how many advanced medical degrees he has received from Harvard Medical School and Johns Hopkins.

The motto is this: "Treat your future clients the way you would like to be treated yourself."

How to deal with conference calls with your clients

It is getting more difficult these days to have face-to-face meetings with your clients. In many cases, they have been replaced by cell phones and emails. The two main reasons are time and money. Your client has limited time available for meetings. His budget may also restrict his travels.

If you have scheduled a conference call with your client, you want to make sure that you treat that conference as if it is a face-to-face meeting. Always try to take that call in your office if possible. You want your client to feel that you are totally engaged during that call. If you have scheduled the conference call for a time when you will be on the road or at the airport catching a flight, find a QUIET place to take that call. You do not want your client to hear the airport flight announcements through your cell phone. One possible solution is to take the conference call inside one of those airline VIP lounges. They have quiet meeting rooms that you can rent for a reasonable fee and use as your private office. If that is not possible, take the call inside your car or outside the airport terminal.

Another solution is to activate the mute button on your cell phone so that your client cannot hear the airport announcement. The main benefit of taking any one of the above approaches is that you may not need to tell your client you are on the road since he can't hear the background noise.

It is critical that you prepare for the conference call the same way you prepare for a face-to-face meeting. Talk to your internal team right before the client call to make sure that you are all on the same page and are prepared to discuss critical information and answer client questions on the spot. An informal internal agenda will help keep the call on topic and impress upon the client that your team is engaged and prepared for the meeting

The bottom line is this: Give your client the perception that you are always fully engaged on his project. It is important to him that he feels he has your undivided attention at all times. You may have ten clients; but he has only one consultant and that happens to be you. And that's the only thing that matters to your client.

A project manager was actually fired by a large company because he was always "on the road" or at the airport when he had conference calls with his client. The client could hear the background noise. One time the consultant cut off his client in the middle of a conference call because his flight was boarding. The client felt that the consultant was not fully engaged on the project and demanded his replacement. Remember – what matters most is your client's perception.

Perception is reality.

If you are meeting with your client at a face-to-dace meeting, the first thing you ought to do is turn off your cell phone. NEVER interrupt a client because you need to take a call. Just think about this for a moment. How would you feel if someone puts a hand in front of your face while you are talking and tells you to stop because his phone is ringing?

If you forget to turn off your phone and it rings, apologize to the client, turn it off and ask the client to continue. It sends the correct signal that you value his conversation much more than an incoming call.

Chapter 4:   Marketing in the Internet Age

There are two aspects of the Internet age that affect your ability to make connections with your future clients. These are: how to make use of websites and how to handle your email messages.

Visit Your Future Client's Website

Before making your first contact with your clients, you should visit their organization's website. There is a wealth of information available to you even before meeting with your clients. Find out everything you can about your client's business. Find out how big they are, how they conduct their business, who their customers are, how many locations do they have, etc. The more information you have, the better.

This is in keeping with Aristotle's philosophy on communication: know your audience.

Review their organization's press releases on the website. These news items will give you insights on the latest developments within your client's organization. You can use such knowledge in your conversation with them at your face-to-face meetings later. It is a great ice breaker. And it shows you really care about your client's organization.

Your clients will appreciate the fact that you have taken the time and trouble to find out about them.

Always Google your future clients.

Key Points about Your Website

Many consultants believe that their website is their marketing tool. It is actually much more than that. Your company website is often the first impression that your future clients will have about your operation. Even when someone has recommended your company to your future clients, the first thing they usually do is visit your website. They do that before they make their first phone call to you. They want to know all about you before they talk to you.

Instead of a generic mission statement about how your firm strives to provide the highest quality service to your clients, the focus of your website should have much more specific information.

All consultants say the standard things – they are the best and they provide the high quality services to their clients. They all "deliver value on every assignment." They are all working "to earn their clients' trust." One big firm says it will "do whatever it takes to outperform" its clients' expectations and will "deliver innovative solutions."

What do all these fancy and vague words mean? Notice that not a single word can be put in a wheelbarrow!

What else would you expect your competitors to say? They are all going to say the same thing. You need to show how you are different from the crowd. You need to differentiate yourself from the mob.

When your future clients visit your website, they are looking for answers to the following questions:

Benefits. What are the benefits to them if they hire you?

Experience. Have you worked on projects that are similar to what they have in mind?

Approach. Specifically how can you help them with their problems?

Assurance. What do others say about you? The answer to this question will give your clients a level of comfort that hiring you will not be a mistake for them.

It is all about your clients. Not about you.

If your website can address these issues clearly and specifically, you stand a good chance of getting a phone call from your future client.

Try to use Plain English to describe what you do. Do not load up your website with technical jargons and legalese.

Forget about your "Mission Statement". You should be able to tell your customers what you do in one simple sentence. If you specialize in soil remediation, say "we clean up contaminated sites". This sounds a lot more meaningful and much less contrite to your future clients than some gibberish like "our mission is to provide the highest quality service to all our clients and exceed their expectations with the best price possible throughout the whole world." Just about every consultant has similar platitude on its website.

Here is another mission statement example. Levitz Furniture's mission statement was that they had a mission of "satisfying the needs and expectations of our customers with quality products and services." That wonderful mission statement did not keep the company out of bankruptcy.

So instead of focusing on your generic statement of qualifications, you post specific stories about your different projects. Tell your future clients specifically how you were able to save your clients money. Tell them how you were able to make your clients look good within their organizations and solve their problems, etc. Once you have conveyed this message to your future clients, there will be no need for you to tell them how great you are. They will have known already.

In designing your website, make sure that it is easy for your clients to navigate through it. Do not overload the site with extraneous information. Design the website from the standpoint of your visitors and not from your own standpoint. Here are some practical suggestions:

The design should be succinct and to-the-point.

Try to avoid generic statements or declarations.

Offer a free newsletter or other free information online to give your visitors a reason to keep coming back. Offer free downloads. Your local ice cream shops do that all the time. They offer their customers a free taste of their products.

Avoid large graphic files and pictures that require a long time to open or download.

Make Use of Social Media

Start a blog (weblog) on your area of expertise. You can use your blog to provide updates on regulations for your visitors. You can post how you will solve a particular problem.

A blog is a web log and it means just that. It is a log entry you make on the Internet to share with the world. It comes in many forms: diary, newsletter, news release, editorial, opinion piece or promotion. Most companies and government agencies have blogs of their own. Many environmental organizations or non-government organizations (NGOs) also have their own blogs. Many environmental law firms and consulting firms also have their own blogs where you can download or obtain up-to-date information on current environmental issues for free.

If you have material or news that you want to share with the world, you can start your own blog for free. The two most popular websites that offer free blogs are www.blogspot.com and www.wordpress.com. You will find a following of your blog in a short time.

Twitter. Twitter is a worldwide Internet phenomenon that has exploded over the years in popularity. It even started revolutions in the Middle East recently. If you have your own blog, you want to link your blog to your twitter so that every time you write a new blog entry, your twitter is updated. You can use URL short cuts to do the linking since you are only allowed 140 characters for every twit you write.

Facebook. Facebook started as a private social connection site for students at Ivy League universities. It is now the largest Social Media network in the world. You can set up a Facebook account for your company and promote your products and services. As a social medium for professional service providers, Facebook is not the best venue. It is geared more towards retail establishments.

LinkedIn. LinkedIn is by far the most useful Social Media tool available to the environmental professionals. It is designed for business people to connect and share information with one another. Once you have joined LinkedIn (for free), you can invite all your business associates and friends to join your network simply by importing their email addresses into LinkedIn. They become your connections once they join your network. You can then share ideas with them and the rest of the millions of members through discussion groups. There are numerous environmental groups you can join.

Here are just a few discussion groups: Environmental Trainers, Association of Environmental Professionals, Carbon Market Business Networks, Environmental Issues in Business Transactions, Consultants Network, EHS Professionals, Environmental Analyst, Environmental Compliance and Enforcement, Environmental Compliance Auditors, Environmental Consulting Professionals, ISO 14001 EMS, Sustainability, Environmental Engineers Group, Manufacturing Operational Excellence, Society of Environmental Engineers, etc. The list goes on and on.

Once you belong to a group, you can participate in its discussions or you can initiate your own discussion group. You will learn how other professionals handle a particular environmental situation. You can offer your opinion on any given topic. You can ask others for advice or opinion if you come across a situation you are not sure how to handle. If you don't see a group you want to join, you can start your own group.

For example, in the Environmental Issues in Business Transactions Group, you will learn how environmental attorneys and consultants handle particular due diligence issues in property transfer. You will be updated on the latest court decisions. There is a treasure trove of free information and it is all there for the taking if you are willing to spend a bit of time searching.

YouTube. This is the world's most popular video sharing site run by Google. Many companies and government organizations post their videos on YouTube. For example, If you type in "Chemical Safety Board" on YouTube, you will find many of the Board's safety videos there. The U.S. Chemical Safety Board investigates major chemical accidents. It's videos discuss the findings of the Board and are excellent training material and resources for preventing future accidents.

You can link your twitter and your blog to your LinkedIn account and imbed YouTube videos in your Facebook page and blogs. The world is one giant spider web of information sources. That's why it is called the World Wide Web.

Email Handling Etiquettes

It is important that you properly manage your email communications with your clients. Keep in mind that your clients are probably inundated with email messages at work. You should always ask your client about his preference on how he wants to communicate with you. Ask if he prefers emails or voice mail?

The cardinal rule about email is this: If yo do not want something to be memorialized forever in cyberspace, do not put it in an email and send it. Once it is out there, it is pretty much out there forever.

Do not get into the habit of forwarding emails to your clients without adding your comments or notes. You may have a habit of forwarding jokes of questionable taste to all your friends via emails. That's fine. But do not do that with your clients! And never forward any emails from your client to another person without your client's permission. Your client's email to you is for you only and his email address is private. You must always respect his privacy.

Here is an example: Your colleague has sent you an email offering a solution to your client's problem and you would like to "pass it on" to your client. You forward the email to your client with the following comment: "Here is what John from our office has suggested about resolving your issue. I agree with his assessment and possible solution. Please take a look at it and let me know when is a good time for me to call you to discuss this." This email handling procedure is good because it shows your client that you are engaged in his situation and that you have taken the time to "talk" to him in the forwarding email. It is much better than simply forwarding the email without any comments.

Always reply to your client's email in a timely fashion. Never take more than a day to reply to an email. It is just rude if you ignore your client's email. Emails from your clients to you are just like telephone messages. They are a call for you to do something. If your client sends you an email jsut to provide you with information, acknowledge it with a short email that says: "Got it...thank you". It only takes a few seconds to do that. Ignore your client's emails at your own peril. When you do reply to your future client's email, make sure you always include the original email from him so that he has a continuous paper trail.

Another helpful hint when emailing your clients is to include specifics in the subject title of the email so that your client can easily determine if it is something that he needs to address right away or later. For example: a subject that reads "Updated Lab Reports 5/06 – Site B" tells the client more about the email content than an email titled "Lab Reports". Including an action in the subject title is also helpful, such as: "Need your approval – Final Monitoring Rpt. –Site B". When the client tries to find the email at a later date and he has 50 emails titled "Lab Reports", he will appreciate your thoughtfulness.

If you are sending a newsletter or announcement to all your clients, be sure to put their email addresses in the "Bcc" section. That's blind carbon copies. In that way, you are not disclosing all your clients' private email addresses to everyone else unless you have specific permission from them to do so. It is important to respect your clients' privacy.

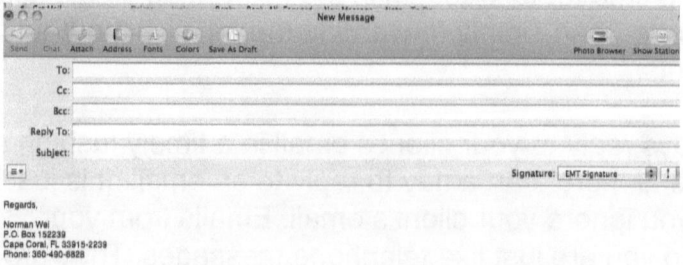

In general, think about all of the things that annoy you

most about emails and make sure you don't annoy your clients with the same things.

Chapter 5: Making Sales Presentations

Presentation skill is by far one of the most critical business development tools. It will make or break you.

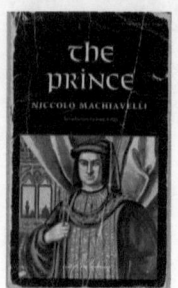

Perfectly well qualified engineers have lost multi-million dollar contracts simply because of a bad presentation.

There are two basic reasons why you make a presentation. The first one is to convey an idea and to inform your audience. The second reason is to convince your audience to do something – like hire you.

One of the biggest challenges facing you during the presentation is people's natural resistance to change. People are always afraid to make mistakes (like hiring the wrong consultant) and be viewed by their colleagues as having made an error of judgment.

Machiavelli stated it best in his book "The Prince" that resistance to change is human propensity throughout history:

"There is nothing more difficult to carry out, nor more doubtful of success, nor more dangerous to handle, than to initiate a new order of things. For the reformer has enemies in all those who profit by the old order, and only lukewarm defenders in all those who would profit by the new order, this lukewarmness arising partly from fear of their adversaries - and partly from the incredulity of mankind, who do not truly believe in anything new until they have had actual experience of it."

Another important aspect of presentation is that it should be short and to the point. It should also allow ample opportunity for the audience to ask questions throughout the delivery. This gives the clients the feeling of being part of the process and not just being sold to.

Always get off to a fast start. Do not spend the first 5 minutes talking about yourself or your firm. If you find yourself in front of a panel who is prepared to spend an hour listening to your presentation, chances are that they already know about your firm. What they don't know is how your firm will help them. Get to the gist of your presentation within the first minute. Tell your audience right away what you plan to tell them. Focus right away on your clients' problems and your solutions.

Give as many practical real-life examples as possible in your presentation. That's how your audience is going to relate to your presentation.

You want to communicate enough information to your audience to take you to the next step. It is not necessary for you to communicate every excruciating details of your proposal in an oral presentation. Your future clients can read the details later if they wish to. But if you bore them to tears with the details, they may not want to read your proposal. Just focus on the absolute essentials.

NEVER give a copy of your PowerPoint slides to your audience. And NEVER give them your presentation material at the beginning of your presentation. Why? The minute you hand out your slide presentation to the audience, they will start reading it. Many will skip ahead of you. Since people can read a lot faster than they can follow you, they will be reading your last slide when you are still talking on your second slide. The worst part of it all is that you will have lost the audience's attention. They are no longer listening to you. They are wondering what those bullet points mean on slide #15. It is a recipe for disaster.

Have you ever wondered why the movie theaters do not provide you with a complete story line of the movie you are about to watch? They don't want to give away the ending!

Instead of leaving your client a copy of your slide presentation, you give them a written document that has all the points you have made in your presentation. A document with full sentences and connected thoughts - not a bunch of talking points. Give them an Executive Summary of your presentation on several pages with full sentences and paragraphs. Your Executive Summary is your first step towards a contract with your future clients. It provides the framework on the scope of your work. Contracts are never written in bullet points.

Many consultants – in trying to tell the entire story at the presentation – end up cramming all the details in their slides and making them totally unreadable to their clients.

Interaction with your client is very important. You should use the presentation to help move the sale process along while giving your client the chance to ask questions and for you to find out more of your client's requirements. Never make a presentation for the sake of making a presentation. It doesn't matter how slick your slides are; the presentation will fail if the interactive elements are absent.

Also try to arrange for your presentation to be the last one – after all your competitors have gone through theirs. It will give you a distinct advantage.

Try to dress appropriately for the presentation. That means matching the attire of the audience. If you are making a presentation to a group of senior executives who are all in three-piece business suits, you should be similarly attired. But if you are presenting your proposal to a group of engineers who have their shirt sleeves all rolled up, you do the same.

Attorneys are notorious for ignoring the audience when it comes to dressing appropriately. They are almost always over dressed – making them look stiff and arrogant when everyone in the audience is in casual wear.

If you are not sure about the dress code before the meeting, it is safer for you to be a bit overdressed because you can always take off your jacket, undo your tie and roll up your sleeves.

A few words about formal presentation: There is an interesting story that Lou Gerstner told in his book "Who Says Elephants Can't Dance". Lou is the former CEO of IBM who turned the behemoth around.

In other words, he made the big elephant dance.

At an important meeting, as one of his executives was making a formal presentation on an overhead projector. Lou simply stepped to the table and, as politely as he could in front of the presentation team, switched off the projector. After a long moment of awkward silence, Lou simply said to the staffer, "Let's just talk about your business." Lou Gerstner mentioned this episode because it had an unintended, but terribly powerful ripple effect throughout IBM.

Formal presentation is just one of the many ways for you to convey your message to your audience.

Making Your Ideas Stick

Whether you are a consultant, architect, contractor, salesman, realtor or attorney, you will need to sell a new idea to your client or customer at some point. For you to make your ideas stick with your client or customer, you need to have the following elements:

1. Your idea must be presented in a **simple** and easy to understand manner. People must be able to grasp your new idea quickly.

2. It must be **specific** in nature. You must give your audience enough specificity to be able to visualize or conceptualize your idea.

3. It must have an element of **surprise** to it. To get the audience's attention, your idea should contain an element of surprise.

4. It must appeal to the **emotion** of your audience. It is important for your audience to relate to your idea through its own emotional road map. In other words, the audience needs to feel a sense of excitement about your idea. It should feel good about it.

5. It must be told in the form of a **story**. The best salesmen are excellent story tellers. Every presentation involves telling a story.

One final point: For your idea to take hold, you must have credibility. For the audience to accept your idea, it must believe that you have credibility. The term credibility is not just restricted to academic achievements or related experience. It includes likeability. The audience needs to "like" you in some manners before it will even began to listen to your ideas. It is human nature that people like to deal with people they like.

Below are some examples:

On May 25, 1961 President John F. Kennedy delivered a speech before a joint session of Congress in which he stated that the United States should set as a goal the "landing a man on the moon and returning him safely to the earth" by the end of the decade. He told the story of how the Soviets had jumped ahead of the U.S. in space exploration and he appealed to the patriotic emotion of the law makers and country to fund the space program.

The concept of "landing a man on the moon and returning him safely to the earth" is simple and straight forward. Anyone can understand and visualize it.

What if President Kennedy had said this: "It is our plan to go before Congress to request a significant increase in the budget for our inter-planetary exploration program to enable a space module to be placed on the lunar surface in the foreseeable future." What would have been the country's reaction to this? Probably with a big yawn.

Here is another example: A plane manufacturer puts out a release that says: "We plan to make the best passenger plane ever built in the world". How will the audience take to this idea? What does "best" mean?

If the aircraft manufacturer says this: "We are going to build a plane that will have 200 comfortable seats, can fly 5,000 miles nonstop and need no more than a mile of runway to land. The noise level at takeoff will be 90% lower than the quietest plane currently flying to-date. " From this description, the audience has a much better appreciation of what kind of new plane it is going to be. The announcement is specific and it appeals to the emotional needs of the audience. It also contains high quality information.

The book "Made to Stick – Why Some Ideas Survive and Others Die" by Chip Heath and Dan Heath is a very interesting book on selling ideas to an audience.

Preparing for the Presentation

Conventional wisdom says that you should always rehearse, rehearse and rehearse your sales presentation. And many consultants follow this wisdom.

Yes, rehearsal is good. But you need to do much more than that. And be aware that over-rehearsal can diminish your chance of success. It can work against you. A combination of knowledge and preparation is a much better strategy. You should go over how you are going to make your presentation. Go over in your head how you will deliver the presentation. You want to make sure your slides are in the proper sequence and well organized.

Decide beforehand how much time you are going to spend on each slide.

But NEVER, NEVER memorize your presentation!

The rationale for rehearsing your presentation is this: It gives you a sense of security because you will know the sales pitch by heart. (Some may say it is a false sense of security). You know when to pause for effect. You know exactly where in your presentation to turn over to your other team members. It ensures a smooth presentation.

In reality, the critical factor a client looks for in any presentation is NOT just how smoothly it goes. It is fine to be smooth. The buyers (in most cases, the end users - the engineers or the managers) want to make sure you – the consultants – know what you are talking about. They want to make sure you know the substance – rather than the form. They want to be sure that you can solve their problems in a timely and cost effective manner. More important, they want to make sure that they are making the right purchasing decision by selecting you.

Sometimes an overly slick presentation may backfire on you. It all depends on the audience. If you are presenting your ideas to a group of engineers or accountants, they may want to see a lot of details and numbers. Slickness may turn them off. They may think you have something to hide from them. On the other hand, if you are representing your ideas to senior management, they may only want to see the overall big picture and not be too concerned about the details.

Never memorize your presentation word for word and think that you are ready before the audience. Given enough time, anyone can memorize a presentation on Einstein's Theory of Relativity and go before a group of theoretical physicists and make a smooth presentation – until someone asks a question that the presenter has never thought of!

You don't want to spend all your time rehearsing the delivery of the sales pitch. You should always focus your time and energy on understanding the subject of the presentation.

Do not allow form to take over substance. There is nothing that will save you from a disaster if you do not know your topic.

Before you make a big sales presentation, you should assemble your team and go through the process of identifying every possible and imaginable question that might be asked during the presentation. Once you have identified these questions, you should then take the time to formulate the answers and try them out on the team members. This Q & A session should make up a big part of the "rehearsal". Your answers have to make sense to your future clients. The point you want to get across to the clients is that you are the expert they need to retain. And remember - they are not looking for smooth talkers or orators. They are looking for consultants to solve the problems they have on hand. They are looking for your approach to solving their problem.

Do not substitute delivery for knowledge.

In Frank Luntz's book "Words That Work", he lists ten rules of effective language. We can apply these rules in our presentations. Frank uses advertising slogans to illustrate his points:

1. **Simplicity**. Try to use small words whenever you can. Forget about fancy multi-syllable words.

2. **Brevity**. Try to use short sentences if you can. Nike's "just do it" ad campaign is a good example. Have you noticed that most executive office memos are only one page long and have short sentences. No one wants to read a 200-word paragraph.

3. **Be credible**. A good example is Wal-Mart's slogan "Always low price. Always". That's way it is for the world's largest retailer.

4. **Be consistent**. The rental car Avis's campaign "We try harder" was launched in 1962 and the company has stuck with it for more than four decades. The consistency of this message has helped Avis to cement its position as the second-biggest car-rental company in the world.

5. **Offer something new.** Try to get the audience to think in a new way. The success of Volkswagen's think small campaign in the late 1950s was an example of shifting the thought process in a novel way. Apple Computer became the world's largest corporation (in terms of market value) surpassing Exxon Mobil by offering something new to the world.

6. **Sound and texture do matter**. The phrase "snap crackle and pop" immediately conjures up images of the actual sound of the cereal itself. Consumers can hear it.

7. **Personalize your message.** A good example is GE's slogan "We bring good things to life". It personalizes the message.

8. **Visualize.** Paint a picture. A picture is worth a thousand words. M & M's slogan "Melts in your mouth not in your hand" has a strong visual component to it - something we can see and almost feel.

9. **Ask the audience questions**. Try to get the audience to have ownership of your presentation.

10. **Provide context and explain relevance.** Burger King's slogan "have it your way" is a good example of a message that provides context and relevance. This slogan sets Burger King apart from the other fast food chains. This message works because the underlying context and relevance consist of a mass-produced assembly-line food production.

Delivering the Presentation

Another area to which you should pay special attention is how you physically present your material. If you are planning on making a computer slide presentation, please make note of the following points.

There are many sophisticated computer software programs that will allow you to present your slides with all sorts of bells and whistles. Like most people, you will be mightily tempted to include all those great animation features such as words flying in and out of each slide from every which direction. Resist that temptation! You want to keep the slides simple. No more than ONE main point per slide. And try to stick with two basic high contrasting colors so that the audience can actually see your material.

Slides that contain too much graphics/animation and too many different colors are not effective communication tools. The essence of the presentation is lost in the special effects. When that happens, the audience will be focusing on the animation rather than your talk. If you must animate something, animate your body rather than your graphics.

You want your audience to focus on your message rather than the special effects. The first sentence in any presentation sets the tone for the rest.

One of the best business books on making presentation is "The Art of the Start" by Guy Kawasaki. Guy is a venture capitalist and he has listened to hundreds – if not thousands – of PowerPoint presentations from entrepreneurs looking for venture capital for their ideas. One of the many excellent recommendations he gives in his book is that you should provide enough details to show you can deliver and enough "aerial view" to show you have a vision. By aerial view he means overall perspective.

People looking for money from venture capitalists are not much different from consultants looking for the next assignment. In his excellent book, Guy also advocates the 10/20/30 rule of presentation. He suggests that all presentations be limited to no more than 10 slides to be given in 20 minutes and with fonts no smaller than 30 points. You get the general idea.

In a sales presentation where you have more time allotted to you, you should use as many slides as you need. But ALWAYS one idea per slide. The time you spend on each slide will depend on the time you need to explain that particular idea or concept.

The horrible habit of people jamming 10 or 13 bullet points onto a single slide came from the days when people had to have their slides made into 35 mm slides. To minimize cost, people jammed as much information as possible onto a single slide. But now you can have as many PowerPoint slides as you need and there are no additional costs involved. Old habits die hard.

There is a growing body of cognitive research that shows that if your presentation contains more than one or two main points per slide, your message is lost to the audience. People cannot handle such information overload. Cliff Atkinson's book "Beyond Bullet Points" is an excellent discussion on how best to present your message to your audience with your PowerPoint slides.

There is a separate section in this book on how to make effective PowerPoint presentations.

First and foremost, you should never read off the slides. Many consultants – not wanting to leave anything out – would pack in a whole paragraph of text onto a single slide and then proceed to read off it. This is a bad mistake. Nothing irritates your future clients more than sitting through an hour-long presentation with a parade of consultants reading verbatim off a series of unreadable slides.

If you know your subject matter well enough – as indeed you should - you ought to be able to speak off your talking points without a prepared script or notes. What you are doing is in effect carrying a normal business conversation with your future clients. You are speaking from your heart and your knowledge base. That is THE most effective way of connecting your knowledge of the subject with your clients. Of course, this approach is very risky if you don't know the subject of your presentation like the back of your hand. But it is extremely effective if you do.

To sum up: You should always speak from your knowledge base and your heart – rather than a bunch of busy slides. To do that, you have to really know the subject at hand.

Handling Questions during the Presentation

This is one area where the really good consultants shine. You need to be sure that you are able to answer questions quickly and with confidence. The best way to achieve this is to do your Q and A preparation as discussed earlier. Try to think of all the possible questions that will likely come from the audience at the presentation. Make sure all your team members know the answers. Also invite your audience to ask you questions DURING your presentation. Tell them they do not need to wait till the end to ask you questions. Why? It makes your presentation more like a conversation than a recital. Besides - if your client has an important question to ask about your presentation, why should he have to wait till the end to ask it?

There should always be a lead presenter at the session whose job is to be the traffic cop – directing questions to the appropriate team member to answer. He is also responsible for making sure that the answers fit the questions. He needs to observe the clients and judge their reaction to the answers. For example, if a team member's answer becomes too lengthy or too technical or both, the team leader should intercede and complete the answer quickly.

The project manager being proposed should be the lead presenter unless he is not comfortable with that role. In which case, a different lead presenter should be appointed.

Here is an example of a presentation gone awry:

Several years ago, the partner of a large South African engineering firm, Bill, flew to London to make a presentation to a group of European managers who had just been assigned the responsibility of expanding a wastewater treatment plant on an island off the coast of South Africa. This particular firm certainly had the expertise to design the treatment plant. It also had the added location advantage over all other competitors due to its proximity to the client's site. And its cost structure was quite competitive.

Unfortunately for Bill, his delivery at the London meeting was hesitant and circumspect. At one point, he paused during his presentation to refer to his written proposal when one of the managers – his future clients – asked him a specific technical question. From that point onward, the entire panel simply sat in the room and listened passively and politely to his presentation. No one asked him any more questions. As soon as Bill left the room, the panel members immediately started to question his capability and qualifications. They had lost confidence in Bill simply because of that one bad impression.

In essence, Bill had 20 minutes to make a first and lasting impression after making a 1,000-miles journey at his own expense. He made a bad impression and ended up losing the job that he should have won.

Here is another example of a presentation gone wrong:

The client was a major city interviewing consultants who were looking to win a big contract. The selection panel gave the four consulting firms a tough assignment. It consisted of five design/engineering questions and the city did not give the consultants much time to prepare. The interview/presentation was limited to one hour for each consulting team. At the interview, three of the teams rose to the occasion. They focused on the questions and put together drawings, charts, and diagrams, and provided detailed solutions to the problems posed by the client. The fourth consulting team spent too much of the limited time talking about the global reaches of its company and all of its capabilities even though the same information had already been included in its written submission to the city.

In the debriefing session, the client told the fourth consulting team that it expected the consultants to do a quick introduction of its team members and then roll up their sleeves and focus on presenting their solutions to the city's problems. It was quite apparent that the three other firms "got it" and exceeded the city's expectations. The fourth team did not win the job.

Chapter 6: Special Tips on Making PowerPoint Presentations

PowerPoint by Microsoft has become the de facto tool that most consultants use for making presentations. Unfortunately, many consultants fail to use PowerPoint in an effective manner. The most common error consultants do is to load up their slides with bullet points and/or text that the audience can barely read from afar.

Do not confuse your PowerPoint presentation with your written proposal. They are not the same. Your proposal should contain all the details of what you plan to do for your clients written out in complete sentences and paragraphs. Your proposal should describe your firm's capability, your understanding of the client's problems and your proposed approach to solving those problems.

The biggest mistake many consultants make is to try to use PowerPoint to present their entire proposal by

cramming 10 bullet points on each slide to summarize all the technical details. The end result is a distillation of some important information that will inevitably be lost in the hierarchical structures of the bullet points.

A classic example of the misuse of PowerPoint can be seen as a result of the following tragic incident.

When the Columbia space shuttle broke up in re-entry to the Earth's atmosphere in 2003, the President appointed the Columbia Accident Investigation Board (CAIB) to look into the causes. As part of the investigation, the Board looked into how those engineers and contractors at the National Aeronautical and Space Agency (NASA) transmit their technical information to their management. The Board observed that "generally, the higher information is transmitted in the hierarchy, the more it gets 'rolled up,' abbreviated, and simplified. Sometimes information gets lost altogether, signals drop from memos, problem identification systems, and formal presentations. The same conclusions, repeated over time, can result in problems eventually being deemed non-problems".

The Board also found that one avenue by which information gets "rolled up" and confused, was through the technology of PowerPoint presentations.

When NASA discovered that a piece of foam had fallen off the shuttle during take off and had impacted its wing, a team of engineers and scientists began a series of analyses to assess any risk that such impact would have upon re-entry. The concern was that the damage done to the wing during take off might impair its ability to withstand the tremendous heat that would be generated when the shuttle began its re-entry into the Earth's atmosphere. That turned out to the fatal cause of the incident.

On Day Nine of the mission, the engineering team presented the results of its risk assessment findings to NASA management in a PowerPoint presentation while

> **Review Of Test Data Indicates Conservatism for Tile Penetration**
>
> - The existing SOFI on tile test data used to create Crater was reviewed along with STS-107 Southwest Research data
>   - Crater overpredicted penetration of tile coating significantly
>   - Initial penetration to described by normal velocity
>   - Varies with volume/mass of projectile(e.g., 200ft/sec for 3cu. In)
>   - Significant energy is required for the softer SOFI particle to penetrate the relatively hard tile coating
>   - Test results do show that it is possible at sufficient mass and velocity
>   - Conversely, once tile is penetrated SOFI can cause significant damage
>   - Minor variations in total energy (above penetration level) can cause significant tile damage
>   - Flight condition is significantly outside of test database
>   - Volume of ramp is 1920cu in vs 3 cu in for test

the shuttle was still in space. One of the critical slides used in the presentation contained six levels of hierarchy.

According to the Board, important engineering information was either "filtered out or lost in the small prints within the bullet points."

The CAIB concluded: "When engineering analyses and risk assessments are condensed to fit on a standard form or overhead slide, information is inevitably lost. In the process, the priority assigned to information can be easily misrepresented by its placement on a chart and the language that is used. . . . As information gets passed up an organization hierarchy, from people who do analyses to mid-level managers to high-level managers, key explanations and supporting information is filtered out. In this context, it is easy to understand how a senior manager might read this PowerPoint slide and not realize that it addresses a life-threatening situation. . . . The Board views the endemic use of PowerPoint briefing slides instead of technical reports as an illustration of the problematic methods of technical communication at NASA."

PowerPoint as a Visual Tool

One of the key points to remember is that presentation is more about inspiration than information.

You are trying to inspire your future clients to hire you. Details of your proposal are already in that half inch thick three-ring binder on the desk in front of your client.

When you open up your word processing program, the screen is usually in portrait format – just like a book or your technical proposal. On the other hand, the PowerPoint screen is always in landscape format. In other words, the width of the screen is always larger than the height. It is just like your TV screen or the movie you watch in a theater.

Why is that?

Because PowerPoint is a visual communication tool. It is **not** a written communication tool like your proposal.

That is precisely the reason why you should never cramp your PowerPoint presentation slides with words. Visuals work a lot better in landscape format. That's why movies do not have words written all over the screens. Subtitles are all they have.

The most effective way to do a presentation is to tell a story by framing the setting, identifying the protagonist, describing the action, and offering an ending.

Just like a Hollywood movie. You are telling a story.

The key point to remember is that much of the presentation will be done by the presenter's narration. The headlines and graphics in each slide provide only the visual impact and backdrop for your story telling. Your story is not a novel because you do not need to spend a lot of words describing the setting. The visuals in your slides do that for you. Your presentation is really more like a movie script supported by PowerPoint's graphics and visual effects.

For the audience, it is like watching a movie or documentary with you as the narrator – going from scene to scene.

In your slide presentation, each slide should contain only one complete sentence (that's the headline) and it should be supported by simple graphics or photographs that reinforce the message contained in that single headline. The headline should be written in conversational tone.

Research in multi-media presentation has shown that given this format, your audience will quickly scan the headline and sit back and pay attention to what you have to say. This is a much more effective way for you to communicate your ideas to the audience than to have them dart around ten bullet points or trying to read a massive amount of text on the screen.

Dr. Richard Mayer, a well-known authority on multi-media research and Professor of Psychology at the University of California in Santa Barbara, has done extensive research in the field of multi-media presentations. His findings can be summed up as follows:

> 1. *Multimedia Principle:* Students learn better from words and pictures than from words alone.
> 2. *Spatial Contiguity Principle:* Students learn better when corresponding words and pictures are presented near rather than far from each other on the page or screen.
> 3. *Temporal Contiguity Principle:* Students learn better when corresponding words and pictures are presented simultaneously rather than successively.
> 4. *Coherence Principle:* Students learn better when extraneous words, pictures, and sounds are excluded rather than included.
> 5. *Modality Principle:* Students learn better from animation and narration than from animation and on-screen text.
> 6. *Redundancy Principle:* Students learn better from animation and narration than from animation, narration, and on-screen text.
> 7. *Individual Differences Principle:* Design effects are stronger for low-knowledge learners than for high-knowledge learners and for high-spatial learners rather than for low-spatial learners.

First of all, forget about all those psychology terms like "Modality Principle", "Coherent Principle", etc. They are just jargon used in the trade to make laymen feel stupid. Every profession has its own set of jargon.

The first finding shows that people learn better (absorb more) from a presentation with both pictures and words rather than just a bunch of words.

The third finding shows that people learn better when the words and picture appear at the same time. That means none of this fading and fading out, zooming in and zooming out, flying in from the side stuff. The more animation you add to your slides, the more DISTRACTED your audience is going to be. If you must show animation, show them a short movie.

The fourth finding tells you to stick to the basics and not to throw a bunch of words (bullet points) on the screen. Narration (you talking to the audience) is a much more effective way to communicate.

Open with Five Slides

The first five slides in a presentation are the most important. They define the story and set out the rest of the presentation. Cliff Atkinson suggests you tell your story this way:

    1. Define the setting (the topic of your story)

    2. Identify the protagonist (main player in your story)

    3. Describe the imbalance (the place where the protagonist finds himself)

    4. Describe the balance (the place where he wants to be)

    5. Offer a solution (how he can get there)

Imbalance is what exists, the balance is what is desired, and the solution is specifically how you propose to bridge the gap between what exists and what is desired. In other words, the imbalance is the problem that your future clients are facing. The balance is what they wish to happen. Your job as a consultant is to show your future clients how you propose to bridge that gap.

Presentation of an idea is really an art. It consists of three components:

Contents. These are the ideas in your proposal.
Composition. This is the right amount of details in your presentation.
Performance. This is how you deliver your presentation.

Each of these three components is a necessary but not sufficient condition for success in conveying your idea to your clients. All three must be present and done well for you to succeed. A good outcome will only happen when all three components are done well.

A presentation with good contents and composition but poor performance will yield a bad outcome. Your clients will either not understand your great ides at all or if they do they will say to themselves: "Well, the ideas seem fine but we don't much care for the presenter."

A presentation where all three components are bad will of course result in rejection.

A presentation with bad contents and composition but excellent performance will likely get this response: "Well – we don't care much for the ideas but he seems likes a nice fellow." Another rejection will be sure to follow.

In other words, your performance at the presentation can be no better than the material you are presenting. But good material or ideas can be easily ruined by bad performance. And this happens often.

The Three Main Points of Presentation

You can use as many slides as you need in your presentation. But make sure you present only ONE point per slide. The bad habit of jamming 12 bullet points in a single slide really started some 30 years ago when people had to pay someone to make 35mm slides for their projector. And the cost was $3 or $4 per slide. So people jammed as much information as possible into a single slide in order to save money.

Remember: You can now make as many PowerPoint slides as you need. They are all FREE!

If the job you are seeking is highly technical in nature, the details of the content should be in your written technical proposal.

Using the principles described above, here are 5 simple slides prepared for a proposal to perform environmental audits for a multi-national corporation.

The 5 slides frame the story by describing the setting, identifying the protagonist, outlining the imbalance and balance and offering a solution.

Slides	What your slides are doing
 Environmental laws allow citizens to sue companies for violations	This slide provides the setting for the story: Congress has enacted environmental laws that allow private citizens to take companies to court if the agencies fail to take enforcement action against the violators. It answers the question "where are we?" for the audience.
 Large companies with violations and deep pockets are most vulnerable	This slide identifies your clients as the protagonist in the story. It answers the question "who are we in this setting?" for the audience. It tells your clients that if they have on-going violations of their permits, they could become targeted.

Slides	What your slides are doing
	This slide shows the imbalance in the story. Those environmental groups could come in and sue your clients and disrupt their business. Your clients are exposed to this imbalance because they have deep pockets and also they have on-going violations.
	This slide offers your clients a way to be rid of the imbalance and return to normalcy. You then start the process of bridging that gap.
	This slide provides a possible solution to your client to restore balance. This is the bridge from imbalance to balance.

After these initial 5 slides, you then go on to tell your clients that you have arrived at a solution to solve their problems. This is where you go through the details of your auditing plans with your audience. You can add as many slides as you need but each slide should have only

ONE complete sentence describing a main point of your program. So if you have twenty main points, add twenty slides.

The Vioxx Story (non-bullet points in action)

The following is a very interesting story as reported in the Los Angeles Times on April 19, 2006. It illustrates how powerful a good presentation can be:

A Houston trial attorney who was suing Merck & Co. on behalf of a client who died while taking the painkiller Vioxx hired Cliff Atkinson (the expert who developed this new no-bullet point approach to PowerPoint presentations) as a consultant to help with his opening statement in the case. They generated a 253-slide presentation that was so mold-breaking and riveting for the jury that it was dubbed "CSI: PowerPoint" by the media. They used the 253-slide presentation as a very powerful storyboard to tell a story in the place of just presenting a long list of bullet points.

The slides provided very powerful visual impacts on the jurors. For example, instead of saying that the defendant's marketing strategy overpowers obstacles, the attorney showed a picture of a steamroller and then said it. This combination of verbal and visual effects helped drive the message home.

The attorney started by referring to the drug company's executives as "Desperate Executives" - after the TV show "Desperate Housewives". He then used simple slides (one point per slide with appropriate graphics) to illustrate that the company was desperate to rush an unsafe new drug Vioxx to the market because its existing pipeline of drugs was running dry. He told a compelling story to the jurors.

In contrast, the defense attorney "read much of his presentation and illustrated it only with hard to read excerpts from documents whose meaning was shrouded in medical jargon."

According to the newspaper, reporters covering the trial singled out the slides, with one reporter calling them "frighteningly powerful." The trial jurors apparently agreed: They awarded the plaintiff's family $253 million – which worked out to be $1 million per slide!

The jurors not only paid attention, they remembered the presentation!

Here is another example of how to use the first 5 slides to open a presentation:

Slides	What the slide is saying
A big client is looking to hire a new consultant	This is the setting of the story.

Slides	What the slide is saying
It is now your turn to make your sales presentation	This slide identify the protagonist - the person who will be making the presentation.
Your audience may fall asleep during your presentation	This is the problem faced by the protagonist. This is the "problem state"
You want your presentation to stand out from the crowd	This is the solution to the problem. The place where the presenter wants to be. This is the "solution state".

Slides	What the slide is saying
Stop using those Bullet Points will get you there	This slide shows how you can go from the problem state to the solution state. If you stop using those dreadful bullet points, your audience will not fall asleep.

Here is another example on how to start your presentation with the first 5 slides. Let's say you are a bridge contractor and you are trying to convince the government to build a new bridge to ease congestion:

Slides	What the slide is saying
The Tacoma Narrows Bridge is the only bridge to the Olympia Peninsular	This is the setting of the story. There is only one bridge between the main land and the Olympia Peninsular in the State of Washington.

Slides	What the slide is saying
The Washington State DOT (WSDOT) is responsible for the traffic flow Washington State Department of Transportation	This slide identify the protagonist - the agency that is responsible for managing traffic flow on the bridge.
Traffic over the bridge was very congested 	This is the problem faced by the protagonist. The bridge traffic is terrible. This is the "problem state"
 WSDOT would like to reduce the congestion	This is the solution to the problem. The place where the protagonist wants to be. This is the "solution state".

Slides	What the slide is saying
Adding a new bridge will ease the congestion	This slide shows how you can go from the problem state to the solution state. If the protagonist adds another bridge along side the existing bridge, it would greatly ease the congestion.

After you have presented the first 5 slides, you then go on to use as many slides as you need to present your case to the WDOT that you are the right contractor for the job.

Why PowerPoint Makes Us Stupid?

"PowerPoint makes us stupid". That is a direct quote from Gen. James N. Mattis of the Marine Corps, the Joint Forces commander at a military conference in North Carolina. He of course spoke without PowerPoint. "It's dangerous because it can create the illusion of understanding and the illusion of control," General McMaster said in a telephone interview afterward. "Some problems in the world are not bulletizable."

This 4-star general is well known for his brusque and outspoken comments. But he also subscribes to Aristotle's famous dictum on effective communications: Know your audience. He talks like a marine when he is addressing a group of marines. When he is speaking to diplomats, he uses diplomatic language.

Brig. Gen. H. R. McMaster, who banned PowerPoint presentations when he was a Colonel serving in Iraq likened PowerPoint to an internal threat. He was adamant that those dreadful bullet points not be used in briefings by his staff.

Below is the infamous Pentagon PowerPoint slide that prompted a general to say: "If we can understand that slide, we will have won the war."

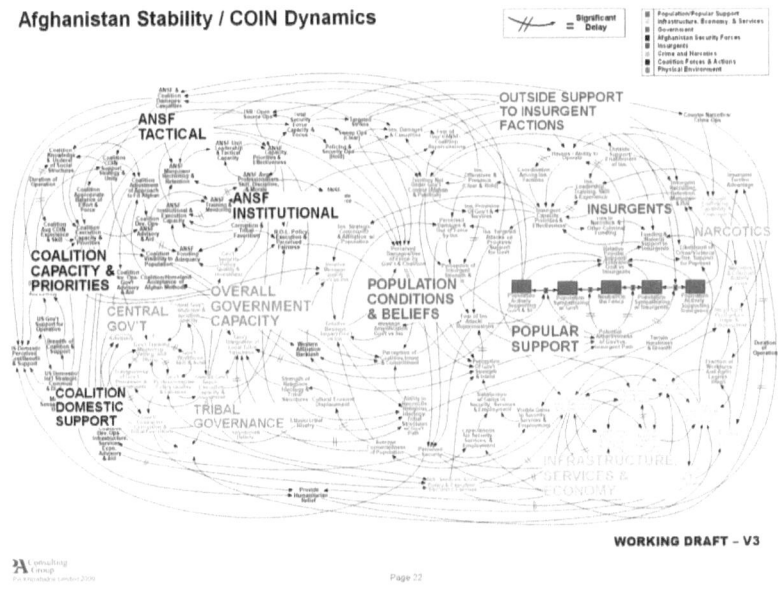

There is a similarly pervasive problem in the business world.

Company executives started replacing written reports with PowerPoint presentations (loaded with bullet points) about 20 years ago. The executive would present slides packed with bullet points at a business meeting. He would proceed to speak at length on each bullet points. That was fine albeit half the audience would be in a semi comatose state by the end of the meeting.

The REAL problem came when the PowerPoint slides were passed on down to the lower level staff for implementation. There were no backup documentations. No detailed analysis. Nada. Since none of these lower level people attended the executive meeting and never heard the presentation, they had no idea as to the nuances embedded in the presentation. All they had was a bunch of notes in bullet points and that's where everything started to go wrong: misunderstanding, misinterpretation, miscommunication, hallucination….etc.

Millions of dollars of mistakes have been made because of this problem.

If you make your sales presentation to your future clients in these bullet points, you run into the same danger of the clients not having detailed documentation of your proposal and approach.

Always back up your oral presentation with a written proposal.

Key points about PowerPoint Presentation

Henry Boettinger is a communication expert who was a senior executive at AT&T. In his book titled "Moving Mountains", he says "presentation of ideas is

 conversation carried on at high voltage -- at once more dangerous and more powerful." This book is by far the best book on how to persuade people to your point of view. All the principles discussed in this book is still valid even it was written back in 1969.

Your PowerPoint presentation is a direct reflection of your ability as a consultant to converse with your future clients. They are going to judge your team's performance based on how well they like the presentation – your story.

Remember that your presentation must include all three key elements: contents, composition and performance.

Here are a few pointers to keep in mind:

1. <u>Show passion in your presentation</u>. It was the German philosopher George Hegel who said: "Nothing great has been accomplished without passion." It is very important for you to show passion when you are presenting your slides. Your future clients need to know that you truly believe in what you are saying and that you have the desire to do the work if they award it to you. They need to know that you have not made the same old boring presentation to 100 other customers and they are now victim number 101. They need to get the sense that your presentation is the most important presentation you have ever made in your career. Your passion must show through. In other words, the best presentations are the ones that carry high voltage. When you

present your reasons for your ideas with passion, the combination will work magic.

In his book "Moving Mountains – the Art of Letting Others See Things Your Way", Henry Boettinger states that "passion and reason can cut through the fabric of doubt, inertia and fear" that your audience may have about your idea.

Passion and reason are like the blades of a pair of scissors. They go together. Neither one can cut the fabric alone.

2. <u>Focus your clients' attention on you</u>. Do not load the slides down with words that are mostly unreadable. Even if they are readable, you should refrain from using them because the text on the screen can be a great distraction to your audience. You want them to listen to what you and your team have to say rather than try to decipher what's on the screen. The best way to get attention is to give it. You want your clients' attention on you. So when you do your homework and demonstrate that you truly understand your clients' problems, you will get attention from your clients.

Another way of keeping your audience's attention is to vary your tone of voice throughout the presentation. Never use a monotone. At various stages of your talk, your tone could go from slow to fast, loud to soft, humorous to serious and melancholic to joyful. Use plenty of interesting and out-of-the-ordinary examples. If you are describing an aerodynamic equation, explain to the audience how it describes the flight of a bumble bee. Examples like that would certain keep your audience's attention on you. Tell stories from your experience that captivate your audience. A presentation does not and should not be dull.

The difference between a presentation with variety and one without is like the difference between a river and a canal. If you are floating down a river, it offers you different surprises at every bend. You may go from farmland to gorges to forest just by floating along. A canal, on the other hand, is a man-made ditch that is straight and not very interesting. A good presentation is a river. A bad one is a canal.

3. <u>Your presentation is not about your ego.</u> It is about your ideas. So avoid reciting your and your team members' qualifications ad nausea. The fact that you are now before your future clients making a presentation means that they already know about you. Or they know you well enough to offer you their valuable time to listen to your ideas. The only time you want to emphasize your team's qualifications is when they have specific relevance to your solution.

4. <u>Don't try to be too clever</u>. There is a quote from Napoleon that pretty much sums up the danger of being too clever. We see that often in bad PowerPoint presentations. The presenter clutters up his slides with all those animations and cheesy clip arts on top of the 10 bullet points. All these special effects do nothing but make the audience dizzy. They distract the audience from the message.

The audience sit there wondering how the next batch of bullet points are going to appear. Are they going to fly in from the left? Or from the right? Or are they just going to dissolve first and then explode? Which bells are going to ring and which whistle will be blown? It is all utter nonsense.

Napoleon once said this: "*The art of war does not require complicated maneuvers; the simplest are the best and common sense is fundamental. From which one might wonder how it is generals make blunders; <u>it is because they try to be clever</u>.*"

Listen to Napoleon! Keep it simple and don't try to be clever.

5. <u>Make sure your presentation is concise and to the point</u>. Sometimes less is better. You want to focus your presentation on the key points and not on some peripheral information. If you focus, you will show your audience that you have taken the extra time and effort to distill complex issues into an understandable format. It gives them a level of comfort in deciding to hire you because they trust you will exert even more effort to solving their problems once you are being paid.

    Do not fall into the trap of wanting to tell them everything about you and your firm and hoping something will stick with the audience. It usually doesn't work that way. All that does is confuse your audience. You will end up with comments like: "What is he getting at?" It is better to repeat a few good points in your presentation than to cover a lot of good and bad points once.

    Many consultants assume incorrectly that their clients equate quantity with quality. They think their clients will feel they are getting their money's worth if the consultants submit a voluminous report. Nothing is further from the truth. There is a very good reason why corporate executives demand one-page memos from their staff. So brevity is the key here.

You certainly don't want your client to describe your presentation as "a tale told by an idiot; full of sound and fury, signifying nothing."

It is not necessary for you to cover all possible combinations and permutations in your proposed solution to the client. Just present enough to make your point. Most speakers pick three main points they want to convey to the audience and stick to them. Why? They have know they have a better chance of convincing the audience of the three points than spraying the audience with 20 points.

Information overload does not work in presentations.

If you are in a cooking contest, do you cook a couple of your best dishes for the judges to decide? Or do you prepare your entire repertoire of 30 dishes and expect the judges to try them all?

Poor speakers try to cover everything under the sun in a one-hour speech because they are fearful that someone will scream out: "Hey, you miss one thing". What you want to do is to employ a technique known as "cognizant omission" used by many professional speakers. For example: You start by telling your audience that you have looked at all possible scenarios and you have narrowed them down to three that are worthy of further discussions. In that way, no one in the audience is going to think that you have ignored or overlooked some salient points of your argument.

And once you feel that you have convinced your audience to your way of thinking, stop pressing the point.

In other words, quit while you are ahead and stop drilling when you strike oil.

Extremely brevity is of course just as bad as excessive verbosity. It forces your audience to guess at what you are trying to say. If you can strike the proper balance between this and verbosity, you will have achieved elegance – a term easier to recognize than to describe. In mathematics, an elegant solution is one that is arrived at with the least number of steps in the least convoluted manner.

6. <u>Remember that a presentation is a "conversation"</u>. You are talking to your future clients about what you plan to do for them. It should not be a monologue. In any conversation, there should be at least two people involved. So try to engage your clients early during your presentation. Get them to talk to you too or at least acknowledge your presence!

The best way to do that is to invite your audience right up front at the beginning of your presentation to interrupt you any time they have any questions – up to a point. You don't want to be spending 10 minutes of your valuable time answering a peripheral question from one member of the audience. But you do want to engage the audience. It is a delicate balance you need to maintain. When your future clients start asking questions, it is a clear sign that they are paying attention to you and they have engaged you and you'd better have some pretty good answers. That's probably why Henry Boettinger used the word "dangerous" in his definition of presentations. This brings us to the next point.

7. <u>Always prepare your team for any anticipated questions</u>. As you go through the rehearsal, ask yourself what kind of questions will your future clients be asking about your presentation? Make sure you have answers to all these questions. If you are going to suggest any new or not-so-well-known technology as part of your proposal, you should know that someone in the audience will have doubts about it. That doubt may linger in his mind throughout the entire presentation and he may not even ask your any question about it. But the doubt will be there. What you need to do is to address any anticipated doubt, concerns or fears that your audience may have before anyone raises them.

For example, you can say: "We understand this is a relatively new technology. However our research has shown that it will work in your situation. Here are some specific case studies of how your competitors have used this technology to great success." The bottom line is that you do not want any doubts to fester in your audience's minds.

Very often, someone in the audience may fear that your new idea or concept may make his own idea look bad. If that is not going to be the case and you sense that fear, you should address it right away and reassure the individual that your new idea is really quite compatible with his. Ease his fear head on so that he can re-refocus his attention on your presentation.

When was the last time you had a conversation with a friend or business associate when you got to talk non stop for 50 minutes before your friend could chime in? You must learn to "listen" while presenting and the best way to do that is to have the audience ask questions DURING your presentation. This is the best way to develop rapport and dialog with your audience. In reality, very few people in the audience will actually ask questions during your 50-minute talk. But the fact that you offer that opportunity to the audience makes them feel at ease, valued, wanted and appreciated.

Also learn to "listen" with your eyes. When you see someone in the audience who has this puzzled look on his face, you know you have lost connection with him and you need to reconnect with him and the rest of the crowd. You do that by asking the audience "Does this make any sense to you?" This will give you a chance to elaborate on your idea and get your point across. If you see someone passed out in a deep coma, you will know your 10 bullet points per slide has done its trick!

8. <u>Be sure to make contact with your audience</u>. The best way to get your message across to your future clients is to establish some sort of rapport or connection. If there is an opportunity for you to meet the audience before your presentation, take full advantage of it. Talk to them. Get as many names as possible and remember them. During the presentation, you can establish connection with your audience by making eye contacts with them. You want them to feel that you are having a private conversation with them.

In the Vioxx trial, it was reported in the press that the plaintiff's attorney "went through 80 slides, rarely breaking eye contact with the jury." Each slide had a picture on it with two or three words. He was able to communicate his thinking verbally to the jury as if he was having a private conversation with each juror. It was also reported that the defense attorney, on the other hand, read most of his opening statement directly from his PowerPoint slides and hardly ever looked up at the jury. There was no connection with the jury.

9. <u>Pay attention to your posture during your presentation</u>. If at all possible, do not spend all your time standing or hiding behind a lectern with both hands firmly grabbing the sides. Stand in front of it or lean against it with your elbow. Walk around it once in awhile if you can. The point here is to have as much

free space between you and the audience. This reinforces the idea of intimacy with your audience. You are having a direct conversation with them.

Remember those Presidential debates? The candidate who does well at these debates is usually the one who takes the trouble to walk out in front of the lectern or into the audience when answering a question by a voter. By doing so, the candidate is seen as making connection with the voter.

10. <u>State the problems clearly and early</u>. The first task you ought to do at the presentation is to clearly state

the problem. If your audience does not see a clearly defined problem, it becomes restless, bored and resentful to your ideas. You identify for your audience a clear description of the problems that you are planning to solve for them. Do not fall into the trap in which many enthusiastic inventors find themselves when presenting their inventions to venture capitalists. These inventors are so excited about their inventions that they jump right in and describe how their new discoveries work. After ten minutes or so of listening to such display of energy, the audience say to themselves or worse yet out loud; "So what?" These inventors fail to tell the audience up front what problems their inventions are designed to solve. They fail to clearly state the problem.

The same bad outcome can befall a consultant if he starts his presentation by telling his future clients how great his company is and how many offices he has in so many countries. The response is also going to be: "So what?" unless that information is really relevant to the problems at hand.

In the 5-slide example shown in this chapter, the stated problem is your clients' potential liability to citizen lawsuits. You state it early on in the presentation and then proceed to offer a solution to minimize your client's liability.

11. <u>Be forceful in your presentation</u>. No client wants to hire a mousy or timid consultant. Whatever you do, don't let them see you sweat. And don't let them sense your fear or nervousness. You may be the world's expert on the topic at hand, if your audience sees you sweat, some of them will think that's because you are not sure of your subject. This

judgment is probably unfair to you. But perception is reality. Your audience will always expect you to have more knowledge than they do on your presentation topic. After all, that's why they have invited you to give them a talk on your ideas. When they sense that you are nervous and seemingly unsure of yourself, they will tune you out and reject your ideas altogether.

Remember that people seldom buy an idea without first buying the originator of that idea. They will judge your ideas by the way you present them.

12. <u>Make sure you maintain continuity</u>. If you have multiple presenters at your meeting with your future clients, you want to make sure that the individual presentations are tied in together and they are coherent. The best way to do that is to insist that each presenter makes specific reference to either the one presentation before or after him. There is nothing more irritating to an audience than to listen to five seemingly disjointed presentations from the same team.

    In general, you should try to keep your team as small as possible. The project leader should be the one to make the bulk of the presentation. If there are specialized area where a particular expertise is required, have the expert in your team speak to it briefly. Do not have a "dog and pony" show and have a cast of ten trooping through the presentation. Some consultants try to use the "dog and pony" approach to show their clients just how well they work as a team. Unless the transitions between the speakers are seamless, your future client is going to think you are doing a school play where every kid gets a talking role and the parents and grandparents get their photo ops.

Make sure your team leader introduces the speakers' topics and ties them together at the end of the presentation. The leader should also be the one to direct questions from the audience to the individual speakers. It is also the responsibility of the leader to make sure that the questions from the audience are answered satisfactorily. You are demonstrating to your future clients how your team will work for them once they hire you.

13. <u>Always start with an opening statement that holds your audience's interest</u>. There are really four subject categories that will perk up an audience. These are: royalty, religion, sex and mystery. As a consultant in the technical arena, your choices are pretty much restricted to mystery.

Using the 5-slide presentation example shown earlier, here is a possible opening statement that will hold the attention of the audience:

"Thank you for the opportunity to speak with you. I would like you all to picture this scene. We are at the reception after a very successful shareholders' meeting of a multinational corporation. The CEO is very pleased that his preferred slate of directors for his Board has been approved by a majority of the shareholders. He and his guests are enjoying the fine food catered by a world famous chef. Just as he is getting ready to go up to the podium to give a speech to thank the shareholders who have supported his slate, a well-dressed man walks up to him and hands him a document. It is a letter from an environmental group giving the CEO 60-day notice that it intends to file a citizen lawsuit against his company for failing to meet his waste water discharge limits in his permit. We are here to present to you a proven way that your company can inoculate against such lawsuits."

This statement sets the stage and offers an element of mystery leading the audience to wonder what that proven inoculation might be.

14. <u>Never read text off your slides and never apologize</u>. There are two things you should never do. You should never read your text out loud word-for-word. And you should never apologize for any short comings that you may think you have in your presentation. It is impossible for many people – except professional actors – who can read a text to an audience and make it sound conversational. Once you start doing that and all your audience can see is a bald head, you lose eye contact with your audience and they get bored.

    You should not apologize because if your apology sounds like false modesty, you audience will notice it and will resent it. If your apology is sincere, the audience will soon find out about your incompetence. Very often, your public speaking style is not as bad as you think because many people are a lot more critical on themselves. So why apologize in advance.

    Many people use bullet points in PowerPoint slides as their teleprompter. The bullet points act as speaking notes to remind them of the topics. That's fine except they forget that people who make speeches with teleprompter don't share their speaking notes with their audience. And that's exactly what you are doing when you flash those bullet points on the screen for everyone to see and read.

There was this business development manager for a large consulting firm who made a presentation at a hazardous waste training seminar. He stood up before the audience and started to apologize for the fact that he was neither an engineer nor scientist and had little grasp of the technical knowledge in his presentation. He then proceeded to read out loud word-for-word 30 pages of text on hazardous wastes that someone had apparently handed him in the morning. And he left the podium. Before he finished, several members of the audience stood up and asked: "Why did we pay $1000 to listen to you read out loud on something you know nothing about?"

15. <u>Try to speak your audience's language</u>. Do not use technical jargons especially if your clients are not engineers or scientists who are familiar with your jargons. You cannot expect your audience to understand and accept your ideas if you speak a language they do not understand. It shows disrespect for your clients and nothing good will come out of it. Even a non-English speaking foreigner who is charged with murder will get a translator to tell him what is happening in court. Why shouldn't your audience get the same rights?

You should also avoid using a lot of acronyms. Experts in their own fields are notorious for doing that. They assume their audience is familiar with those acronyms and pepper their talks with them. An instructor at a seminar on the Clean Air Act did that one time and the entire class was in a near coma after he had used his 15th acronym.

Successful military officers (many 4-star generals) are well known for having the ability to speak their audience's language. When they are addressing their troops in the battlefield, they use language that the enlisted men can understand. When they go before a Congressional hearing or when they are negotiating deals with foreign diplomats, they use a completely different language.

"Speaking your audience language" goes beyond the spoken words. Your attire should be appropriate for the audience. When you are speaking to a group of engineers at a tropical retreat where the dress code is informal, do not show up wearing a three-piece suit. It will just make you look silly and completely out of place. If you are not sure about the dress code at a presentation forum, come dressed in jacket and tie. You always have the option of taking them off to match the audience's attire.

They call it "mirroring" in psychology. You are mirroring the person with whom you wish to have rapport. You mimic the way their speech pattern, their tone of voice, their pace, their mannerism, the way they dress, etc. In reality, we do that all the time. When we wish to speak to a child, we crouch down and speak to the child face to face at the same level. This approach tends to get better results than when we tower over the child and shout out commands.

16. <u>Understand the difference between accuracy and precision</u>. In your presentation, you should use accurate statements with the proper amount of precision necessary to tell your story. The following example illustrates the point. If you are giving direction to someone who is trying to reach the Los

Angeles Airport from San Diego, here are three possible directions:

"You can find the Los Angeles Airport in Southern California." This is an accurate statement but it lacks sufficient precision to be of any benefit to the driver.

"You can get to the Los Angeles Airport from San Diego by taking 405 North and going for 125 miles. There will be signs along the freeway to direct you to the airport." This is an accurate statement with proper amount of precision to get the driver to his destination.

"The Los Angeles Airport is located at 33° 56' N and 118° 24' W. in Southern California." This statement is also accurate but probably has too much precision for the driver. It is not necessary to provide the longitude and latitude.

17. <u>Keep your presentation SIMPLE</u>. Keep it simple and good things will happen. This is one of the many sound advices given in the book "The Power of Simplicity" by Jack Trout. Simplicity is at the heart of many success stories in business. Here are some examples of simplicity at work:

One of the reasons for Papa John's Pizza's success is that it keeps its operation simple. Every location has the same mixer, same water purification system, same oven and same computer system. It makes operation that much simpler for everyone involved.

Southwest Airlines has similar simplicity at work. By flying the same model aircraft in its fleet, it makes maintenance and training much easier. It keeps its spare parts inventory down. The airline has no assigned seating. That makes boarding the plane quicker and it shortens the turnaround time at the gate. That in turn translates to higher utilization rate for its airplanes and greater profit.

Simplicity is key in both examples.

Always present your ideas in bite size chunks. Never lump ideas together . Here is an example:

Will your audience understand you when you present the following to them?

KGBIBMNASACIAFBIAIGEPA

Probably not. It is too large a chunk to digest. Now if you break this into bite size chunks, you audience will understand it:

KGB IBM NASA CIA FBI AIG EPA

Another elegant example of simplicity is something you see everyday on the Internet. Look at Google's search engine web page and you will see simplicity.

There is no clutter. No banner ads. Just type in the term you want to look for in Google.

It is that simple.

Here is what Jack Welch said about simplicity when he was interviewed by the Harvard Business Review in 1989 while he was CEO of General Electric: "Insecure managers create complexity. Frightened, nervous managers use thick convoluted planning books and busy slides filled with everything they've known since childhood……. They worry that if they're simple, people will think they're simple minded. In reality, of course, it's just the reverse. Clear, tough minded people are the most simple."

18. Use common sense in your presentation. Common sense is defined as "native good judgment free from emotional bias or intellectual subtlety." When you are not sure what material to use in your presentation, try to see things as they really are. Don't be too cute or too clever. Use your common sense. If you have that uneasy feeling about including certain material in your presentation, take that as an advice from a friend and don't use it.

19. Limit your corporate overview. Unless your clients specifically ask for it, do not include more than one slide on overview of your company. Many of your future clients are not interested in how many vice presidents you have in your corporate office. They are probably not interested in the history of your firm or your company's mission statement. They are much more interested in how you are going to solve their problems. If they invite you to make a presentation to them, they already know something about your

company. What they don't know is your approach to solving their problems. The only time you should show them how many offices you have throughout the world is when you are bidding on a job that requires global reaches.

20. <u>Use Plenty of Examples</u>. Always give examples and be as specific as you can. Instead of telling your audience what you are saying, SHOW them by way of examples. The fast-food chain Jack in the box has a sustainability page on its website. Most environmental sustainability statements are like mission statements – fuzzy, ill-defined with a bunch of happy talk.

Jack in the box is an exception.

It gives specific examples. It tells the world it has installed smart irrigation controls and low flow kitchen and plumbing fixtures which "could reduce water usage by up to a million gallons a year". It has increased the amount of recycled materials by "more than 20 percent". It has "diverted more than 50 percent" of its corporate office's trash away "from local landfills". It has "decreased electricity usage by more than 7 percent in natural gas usage by 95 percent" at its corporate office. The list goes on. The specific examples with numbers give the audience something to relate to. They can relate to the magnitude of the accomplishment.

Handling nervousness during the presentation

First of all, don't ever let them see you sweat and never start a presentation with an apology .

The best antidote to nervousness is a combination of knowledge and preparation. If you know the topics being presented, you will be able to speak about it with confidence. If you have done your homework and have thought about the questions that might be asked of you at the presentation, you will be less nervous.

Consider this example: What would happen to you if someone handed you some detailed notes on Einstein's Theory of Relativity and ask you to make a presentation to a group of physicists and be prepared to answer any questions on the topic? It would be very natural for you to have extreme anxiety unless you are a physicist and you are thoroughly familiar with the Theory of Relativity. You can stay up all night and memorize the entire theory and the next morning you may be able to give a flawless presentation. But what if someone in the audience asks you a question, will you have the knowledge to answer it?

Memorizing your speech will not help you. In fact, it will make you more nervous. While you are reciting your memorized speech, you will be dreading the moment when someone asks you a question you know you cannot answer.

The moral of this story is that you have to have knowledge of the topic you are presenting.

It is very common to have stage fright. Even accomplished public speakers feel that anxiety pang before getting on the podium. They have butterflies in their stomachs and sweaty hands – just like everybody else.

The nervousness comes from a fear of the unknown – of not knowing how a group of total strangers will react to their presentation. It is a very natural and normal response. All speakers have it. What sets the good speakers apart from the bad ones is that they are able to manage or minimize that fear.

Here are some practical ideas on how to do just that:

1. A very effective way to overcome your nervousness is to think about the last time you accomplished something with great confidence. Relive that moment in your mind. Play it back in your head when you are on stage. Some people have found that if they "anchor" that feeling of confidence to some tangible action like tucking at their sleeves or holding onto a pointer, they can relive that same confident moment during their presentation. Use whatever anchor that works for you.

2. Another very effective way to overcome stage fright is to get to know your audience <u>before</u> you speak. If you are making a sales presentation before a company, try to learn as much as possible about your clients and their organization. At a minimum, get background information about the company. Find out what products it makes or service it provides. It is exactly like going to a job interview. You want to impress your future employer with your knowledge of his company.

   If you know the names of the people on the selection panel, Google them and find out more about them.

The point here is to make yourself feel as comfortable as possible about the people to whom you are going to be presenting. It makes your future clients a little bit less like complete "total strangers" to you. This is the reason many successful public speakers make a point of mingling with the audience before getting up on the podium. It is a great way to overcome the fear of the "unknown".

3. Try to focus on the presentation and not on yourself. Your presentation is not all about you. Remember that your future clients are judging your presentation based on your knowledge and ability to answer their questions. They are not there to rate you as an orator. If you know the topic, you will not be nervous. If you are not familiar with the topic of your presentation, no amount of rehearsal will save you. That's why doing your homework is the key. Knowledge brings confidence and confidence overcomes nervousness.

4. Establish and maintain eye contact with your audience. Speak to them as if they are your colleagues or friends. The more "contacts" – both verbal and non-verbal - you have with your audience, the less they seem like "total strangers" to you. Always treat your presentation as a conversation with your audience. Pick out one or two persons in the audience at a time and make good eye contacts with them and do your presentation as if you are talking to them.

5. Remember that stage fright is most pronounced before you speak. It is a feeling generated by uncertainty. People who are not able to overcome their stage fright often believe erroneously that the fear they have before they speak will get worse once

they get on the podium. The reverse is true. The butterflies in your stomach will fly away and your sweaty hands will dry up once you get into talking about topics that you know so well. Also remember that very often your audience will not even notice how nervous you are. We are often a much harsher critic of our own performance. That's why you should never tell your audience that you are nervous or apologize. Why tell them you are nervous if they don't even know you are nervous.

6. If your lead technical person on the presentation team is too nervous to lead the presentation, you can use one of your most confident and knowledgeable team members as a "Master of Ceremonies" (MC). This person can lead off the presentation and get things rolling, which will settle the nerves of other presenters. The MC can also direct questions and interject, when needed. Special Tips on Making PowerPoint Presentation

Chapter 7: Selling to a Selection Committee

There are still a few organizations out there with selection committees. Most of these are government departments. Some day you may be faced with the task of having to sell to one of these committees. For example, if you are trying to sell your services to a trade association, chances are good that you will be appearing before a committee made up of representatives from different companies in that trade association. Selling to government agencies is the same way.

If you do, watch out. This is by far one of the most difficult tasks – selling your services to a committee.

To be successful in selling to a committee, you really need to sell to each of the members individually. The problem is that each member has his or her own personal agenda. They also have conflicting expectations of you - the consultant. The ideal situation is for you to meet with each member individually to assess his/her individual needs. However, this is often not possible because the members do not want to be bothered with the time-consuming effort or they are not allowed to talk to you. After all, that's why they have a committee in the first place.

In instances where you have a strong committee chairperson with leadership skills, you may have better luck in selling to the group if you manage to develop good personal rapport with the chairperson. But be careful not to offend the rest of the group through your relationship with the leader.

The golden rule is this: If you have it, don't flaunt it.

Don't drop names and brag about how cozy you are with the committee chairperson. This could lead to perception of impropriety and the other members on the committee may resent you. Or they may be jealous of your relationship with the chairperson. You need to tread lightly.

Tactfulness and discretion are the operative words here.

Pricing will be a big factor here especially if you are selling to a government entity with a selection committee. Very often the entity is required by its own rules to go with the lowest "qualified" bidder. So there are two hurdles to jump over: qualifications and price. Most committees are reluctant to deviate from the lower bidder rule because it requires a tremendous amount of paper work to justify going to a higher bidder.

The pricing hurdle is easier to overcome in the private section as long as you are able to convince the committee that you are offering more bang for the buck than the lowest bidder. All you have to do is to convince the committee members that they will not be embarrassed by you.

A Few Words about Politics

Wikipedia.com defines politics as "the process and method of making decisions for groups. Although it is generally applied to governments, politics is also observed in all human group interactions including corporate, academic and religious."

When you sell to any committee, you are dealing with politics - plain and simple. It could be municipal politics or office politics. Whoever is in charge of your proposal must have an acute sense of the underlying politics surrounding the job. He must be able to understand the dynamics involved upon which political decisions are made within the committee. This has little to do with your making political contributions. It has everything to do with knowing the people involved and understanding how they interact with one another.

For example, if you are making a presentation to a municipal government, you need to understand the "politics" or working relationship among the city manager and members of the city council. You need to do your homework and get a true sense of how each council member is going to vote on your proposal. You need to figure out who is the leader of the pack if there is one.

The same is true in the corporate setting. Do not shun "office politics". Do not dismiss it as idle gossip. The successful consultant is the one who is able to handle the "office politics" of his clients. Gossip - when taken in proper context with other information - can provide valuable insights into the client's corporate decision making process. You simply cannot get away from that. Keep in mind that your future clients' decisions are predicated on the "politics" within his office. The more you help him – directly or indirectly - to navigate through his internal mine field, the greater the chance that he will be able to choose you to be his consultant. His main concern is to make sure that whomever he chooses will not make him look bad in his office.

That's just the facts of life.

That's the main reason why many senior partners at accounting firms or law firms are known as rainmakers.

Their job is to schmooze with their existing and future clients and deal with any political situation that may come up. These people live in the real world and they shower their firms with money.

Remember this: It is all about relationships. If you have good relationship with the future client - be it government or private sector - you will have an upper hand in your bidding process. Sometimes - not very often - your future client will tip you off if his organization has already chosen its favorite consultant. That tip can save you a lot of time and money.

Chapter 8: To Bid or Not to Bid

Bidding on jobs and writing proposals can be a very expensive undertaking to any consulting firm. Proposal writing takes your staff away from billable activities. Worse yet – if you get a string of losing bids, it can be very demoralizing to your staff.

You walk into your office Monday morning and find an envelope containing a Request for Proposal (RFP) from a well-known Fortune 100 company that is not your existing client. It looks like a pretty lucrative job and you know you are absolutely qualified to do the work. Should you spend the staff time to prepare a proposal?

To bid or not to bid – that is THE question.

Let's step back and look at why this company is asking your firm to bid on this great job. There are several possible reasons:

They want to find out what other consultants are charging in the current market place so that they can use that as a leverage to bargain with the consultants they are currently using to get a cheaper rate.

They want to hire a specific consultant that they like – but corporate purchasing policy requires that they get at least three separate bids.

They have no intention of awarding the job to anyone. All they are looking for is some free consulting advice.

They are not happy with the consultant they have now and they want to see what other consultants can offer them. They are looking to switch consultants.

They actually have a real need for a consultant and they are eager to find the right one to help them out.

Many environmental managers have used one or all of the above reasons at one time or another for sending out RFPs.

Clearly you don't want to invest your time if any one of reason #1, #2 or #3 prevails.

You would certainly want to take a shot at Reason #4 in order to dislodge your competitor. Reason #5 can possibly give you the best chance at a fair shot at the job.

But how do you know which is the underlying reason?

You need to look at the RFP very carefully.

Be wary if the RFP contains specifications that are out of the ordinary – such as requiring a specific approach or process equipment/design that is not common in the profession. A red flag should go up too if the proposal deadline is unrealistically tight. It is possible that your wired competitor has been working on the proposal for some time and the company does not want the other two bidders to have sufficient time to prepare a good proposal. Sometimes the "chosen" consultant may have actually prepared the bulk of the RFP for the client and included their favored methodology or project approach as part of the specifications.

There was an RFP for training issued by a government agency. In the RFP, the government stated clearly that the chosen training consultant must use a specific book that was written by one of the companies that was also on the bidders' list. Guess which company won the job.

A very effective way to determine if the job has been wired or not is to call up the contact person identified in the RFP and start asking specific questions about the proposal. If the person is vague in his response to you or if he does not even return your calls, that would be a strong indication that the job is wired. It is time to decline the offer to bid.

If either reason #4 or #5 is behind the RFP, you should get a very enthusiastic response from your future clients. It is to their best interest to provide you and all the other competitors with as much information as possible so that they can pick out the best proposal.

When you talk to the company, you want to run through the who, what, why and how routine. You want to find out who the company is and who are the players involved in the RFP. You also want them to tell you who the end users are? You want to find out everything you can about the company. You should start by Googling the company. Look at their website. Read their press releases.

Next comes the what. You want to find out just what specifically are these end users looking for in the proposals and, more important, in the selected consultant. You also want to look for some indication of commitment on the part of the client. What kind of financial resources do they have to fund the project? Or are they simply shopping around for free new ideas? Find out from them what the exact start date for the project would be. Is the start date realistic? Are the goals for the project realistic and attainable? If they are, then that is normally a good indicator of commitment.

Find out if the client is emotionally committed to the project or if he is forced to do it. You also want to determine why they need to hire the consultants in the first place.

You want to find out if the project is a legal requirement such as a settlement from a consent agreement with the government. If it is, you know that the client has to go ahead with it. For example, when a company reaches a settlement with the government as a result of violations of environmental laws, the EPA will often require the company to retain an independent consultant to perform an audit on the operations of the company. This report is part of the settlement terms and must be submitted to the EPA. You might want to talk to the agency staff involved and get as much information as you can about the nature of the settlement.

If the agency is not too forthcoming with you, you can always file a Freedom of Information request with the agency and by law they have to provide you with what they have on file.

If the project is not a result of a settlement, find out if your future clients have in-house capability. And if they do, find out why these internal resources are`not being utilized. You want to determine if there is a real need for your services. In general, there are only two reasons why companies spend money on outside consultants – to solve a problem or to save money. If the reasons don't fit either category, stay away from bidding.

The last question is how they decide on selecting the consultants. What are the selection criteria and who decide?

Ask open-ended questions and be persistent. Get as much high quality information as you can.

There is an old saying in Poker that if you don't know who the sucker is at the Poker table, it is probably you.

The first rule in the consulting business is "never volunteer to write a proposal" for your future clients. If they ask you for one, try to talk them out of it. Prepare a short engagement letter instead that outlines what you plan to do for them – but never offer to do a full-blown fancy proposal with bells and whistles.

With few exceptions, preparing a proposal should be your last resort in business development.

Remember that people buy other people – they don't buy paper.

If you have no choice but to submit a written proposal in order to secure the job, keep the following thoughts in mind:

Keep to the point. Do not use terms like "we are uniquely qualified" and "we provide full service". Everyone knows that there is really no such thing as a "uniquely qualified full service consulting firm". Every consultant makes the same claims. You need to set yourself apart from this crowd. As far as your future client is concerned, the one closest to such billing is probably the firm that is wired to get the job. So forget about such hype.

Always offer some free advice. Now that you have decided to take the plunge, you need to set yourself apart from the crowd by offering your expertise up-front. Remember - you are trying to dislodge your future client's current consultant. So you need to show your future client you really know the stuff. Keep in mind that the first thing most reviewers look at in a proposal is the cost summary page. Now that does not necessarily mean that cost is the deciding factor – most often it is not. The point here is that you want to show your future clients how they will benefit from retaining your services.

Note that this is not the same as bragging about how great you are. Always present your expertise and credentials from the viewpoint of your future clients. It is what your clients think you can do for them that really matters. Always write your proposal from your client's perspective.

Listen. Call up your future client and listen, listen and listen. Find out what your future client is really looking for. Try to identify any hidden agenda or purpose in issuing the RFP. Always ask open-ended questions to elicit meaningful high quality information from your future client. Look for specific information and do not settle for generalities. Try to get your client to open up. Be persistent in your questioning.

The art of eliciting specific information in a conversation is a separate topic by itself. In Chapter 3 on "Looking for High Quality Information", there are some examples of how to ask the right questions. Apply them.

Develop rapport. Develop some sort of personal chemistry with the contact person and/or end user if you can. Without personal chemistry, your proposal is pretty much doomed and may well be dead on arrival. Have you ever wondered why all those big national accounting and law firms have partners who don't seem to do much of anything except play golf with their future and existing clients? They are called "rainmakers" and their main job function is to develop personal chemistry with clients – current and future.

Coup de grace. Get your future client to review your draft proposal with you. If you develop the personal chemistry to the point where you can request that, you are almost there. It is illegal in government procurement circles but this practice is sometimes done in the private sector. At a minimum, you need an inside "sponsor" of your proposal to accord it a fighting chance of winning. The more your future client is involved in your proposal writing process, the greater your chances of success. If your future client wants you to win, he will find a way to help you by dropping hints on how best to develop your proposal.

For those of you who like to take long shots and decide to bid on a potentially wired RFP, here is an approach you could take.

Deviate from the RFP's specifications and give it your best shot. It may well be judged "non responsive" but if you have sufficient intellectual horsepower behind your alternate approach to the RFP's specifications, you just might get your future client's attention. You really don't have much to lose.

Chapter 9: Submitting Proposals

Be wary of any Requests for Proposal. As stated earlier, most companies ask for formal proposals to justify their decisions. In general, don't do it unless you feel you have a fair chance of winning the job.

If you market properly, you shouldn't need to write too many proposals. Many contracts are awarded on a sole source basis regardless of what many corporate purchasing policies say.

Remember that with the down sizing of corporate America, many managers neither have the time nor the inclination to review long written proposals. In general, the higher up the corporate ladder, the quicker is the decision making process. It is not unusual for senior executives to make a $500,000 hiring decision based on a one-page staff memo.

Personal contact is much more effective than a proposal.

So NEVER volunteer to do a proposal if you are already discussing the job with your client. You should offer to prepare an engagement letter for your client to sign.

Remember that sometimes clients use your proposal to justify their decision to select your competitor. Always do your homework before hand and find out why the prospect is asking for proposals. Is he doing it to justify a preferred consultant because his corporate purchasing policy says he has to have at least three bids?

When you are preparing the proposal, try to comply with the RFP's guidelines. If the guidelines do not make any sense to you or if they are detrimental to the success of the project, you should provide your rationale for deviating from the guidelines and provide an improved alternative.

Preparing unsolicited Proposals

Sometimes it may be necessary for you to prepare an unsolicited proposal to your future clients. This happens when you have an idea you want to present to your client and you know he needs a proposal of some sort to process through his own organization to get it approved.

Your "unsolicited" proposal should be very specific to the needs of your client. It should state clearly the benefits to your client, how much it should cost and why he should hire you to do the job. Again – the focus is on your client and not you. You are in effect helping your client sell your idea to his management and get the funding to hire you. So always write the proposal from your client's perspective. That means you will need to ask some very specific questions in order to have some understanding of his internal approval process.

You need to understand your future client's internal "office politics." Tom Peters calls it the "politics of getting things done." You need to understand how things are done in your future client's organization. And then you need to do everything you can to make sure your proposal fits into your client's organizational structure and culture. You are trying to help him sell you to his management.

So always write your proposal from your client's standpoint.

Chapter 10: How to Write Winning Proposals

Nothing tells a client more about you and your firm than the proposal you submit. The content of the proposal and the way you've put it together tell your client the kind of work he can expect from you.

Every proposal has the following three elements:

1. Your client's current situation or problem.
2. Where your client wants to be or the solution.
3. How you plan to help your client get there.

Developing a Theme

Every Request for Proposal (RFP) has an underlying theme. For example, an RFP for a highway extension through a National Forest carries with it the theme of environmental impact assessment to meet requirements set by the National Environmental Policy Act of 1969. Your firm may be the best highway designer in the country, but without emphasizing the theme of environmental protection and presenting your expertise in this area, the chances of landing the job are much reduced.

An example that demands a specific theme was an RFP issued by a major city calling for the development of a master plan for a municipal park. The RFP required three disciplines: land use planning, transportation engineering and public affairs. Special consideration was needed to settle conflicts between land developers and the public.

This is a good example of the "politics of getting things done."

The theme of this proposal needed to revolve around public participation. The winning firm would need to demonstrate that it understood the sensitivity between the public and land developers. It would need to spend a substantial amount of ink in addressing these issues. One of the many possible approaches would be to solicit the affected public on its views and incorporate them in the proposal.

Responding to the RFP

Once a theme has been identified, the next step for you is to earn the right to win the job. RFPs generally contain a Statement of Work or Scope of Work outlining what is required in the project with some specificity. It is not enough to just simply play back the RFP's Statement of Work verbatim in your proposal. Nor is it sufficient to simply state how you propose to arrive at the solutions.

You have to demonstrate to your future clients that your firm has not only studied the problem but also has come up with some specific preliminary solutions. These solutions should be the products of your evaluation of the requirements of the RFP.

They may differ from those suggested in the Statement of Work, but they demonstrate that you are capable of arriving at a possible solution although you may not have all the necessary data. This process allows you to demonstrate the depth of your firm's experience and expertise without having to brag about it. If your firm is confident enough about the technical merits of its solutions and you feel it is a better solution than what is being suggested in the RFP, you should present them as an alternative to those suggested in the Statement of Work.

In other words, don't tell them you can do the job; show them. You want to show your future clients that your company can actually solve the problems for them and let them convince themselves that they truly need your services.

A classic example of the above situation occurred many years ago when a consulting firm was preparing a proposal for a comprehensive environmental monitoring contract in Saudi Arabia. The client agency wanted a monitoring program to determine if the marine ecology in the Red Sea was being adversely impacted by the massive industrial development onshore. The monitoring program would consist of underwater surveillance of marine life, identification of coral species, and laboratory analyses of marine organisms for the presence of industrial pollutants.

The Statement of Work in the RFP demanded a biweekly biological monitoring schedule, which was both impractical and totally unnecessary because changes in marine life and coral species simply cannot be detected during such a short time frame. Such aggressive monitoring schedule would not yield any meaningful data and would be a waste of money.

Instead of blindly following the RFP's demand for a biweekly monitoring program, the successful consulting firm submitted a proposal that offered a quarterly sampling program instead, which was more than adequate for detecting longterm trends. This approach also saved the clients substantial amount of money. The proposal was competitive in price and was judged technically superior since the consultant explained very clearly in the proposal the justification for the reduced sampling frequency. The firm was awarded the multi-million dollar contract.

In effect, you are providing some free consulting work to "sell" your future client. You should make your client think that if he awards you the contract, your firm will be able to start work immediately by refining the proposed preliminary solutions. He doesn't want to award a contract to a firm that has to spend a lot of time learning how to do the job.

While it is important to come up with specific solutions, it is equally important that the proposal be in total compliance with all the specific format requirements of the RFP no matter how trivial they may seem. Some RFPs specifically define the proposal format in terms of headings, etc., which allows them to work from a checklist of evaluation criteria.

To improve your chances of success, you should respond directly to these criteria, and set up the proposal format as specified in the RFP. This will make the evaluation panel's job easier for any side-by-side comparisons. Do not stick with a favorite format of yours; change it to fit your future clients'. Remember: It is simply about them.

Now let's discuss the logistics of proposal preparation.

The key is to prepare an outline listing all the items that require work and assigning specific tasks with strict deadlines to the technical staff. Once you set a deadline, stick with it. Insist that everyone on your proposal team stay on schedule. It is human nature to put off projects until the last minute and then push the panic button. You'd be amazed at the number of firms that meet proposal deadlines by minutes. Some are so late that they have to hire a courier on a motorcycle (to weave through city traffic!) to deliver the proposal to the future clients.

As a matter of good practice, you should strive to have the proposal in final production form at least 48 hours before the submission deadline.

As soon as sufficient technical data become available, you should prepare a working draft so that everyone on the team can have ample opportunity to review and revise the document. But don't overdo the review process. There should be no more than two formal review sessions—the first one to look at the preliminary draft and identify information gaps that need to be filled, and the second to review the final draft for completeness and technical accuracy.

Senior management need not be involved in the actual writing process, but should review and approve the final draft with emphasis on cost analysis.

Also, don't have the technical staff involved in editing the proposal. There is a tendency for technical people to get bogged down with style and sentence structure and forget about the substance they are assigned to produce. Editing should be done after the technical writing has been completed. The technical staff's time can be much better utilized on analyzing the RFP and arriving at the "winning" solutions.

Meeting Internal Deadlines

You should establish realistic deadlines for technical input and stick to them. Once the proposal is in the final review and editing stage, there shouldn't be any more add-ons or late changes from the technical staff unless the changes are absolutely crucial. There is always the temptation to add to and modify the content of the proposal at the last minute. Resist these urges if at all possible.

The truth of the matter is that if the initial planning for technical input is done properly and the schedule is followed, there is really very little to do at the last minute. It is simply not worth jeopardizing the entire enterprise for some last minute and unnecessary detail.

Writing Style

Many proposals tend to substitute bulk for quality. Your proposal should contain only what is needed for your client to review and nothing more. A winning proposal is both concise and precise - it states what needs to be done in a straightforward manner.

You achieve precision by choosing the exact words that convey your thoughts and ideas to the client and nothing more. The readers of your proposal are looking for your solutions to their problems. They are not looking to read a lot verbiage.

Here are several key elements that will help you get your message across.

Be concise. Say what you want to say and no more. Focus on the main issues. Do not over sell.

Tell them why. "I am asking all of you to do this because ...." When people understand your reason behind what you are asking, they may buy into your idea and claim ownership. Once they have ownership, they will be much more willing to accept your idea. No parents ever call their own babies ugly.

Write short sentences in short paragraphs. Keep your paragraphs to no more than 7 or 8 lines. No one wants to read a paragraph that takes up a whole page. There is a reason one-page memos and executive summaries are so common in the business world. If you can't squeeze all your ideas in one page, distill them in an Executive Summary.

If you are discussing a complicated program, you will of course need to attach the details in a separate report.

Use one-sentence paragraphs to emphasis key points.

Keep the tone informal and style conversational. Think of your proposal as a conversation with your future clients.

Do not use a lot of jargons unless you know all your readers are familiar with them. The most successful managers are always the ones who can translate technical (legal, engineering, or financial) terms into plain English for senior management and the public. Your proposal should not read like a Ph.D. thesis unless you are writing a proposal to build a new space shuttle.

Your writing style should ensure clarity of thoughts. Include an "executive summary - whenever the format permits. There must be one person responsible for writing and editing the final proposal. This is particularly important if more than one author is involved in the preliminary drafts. There is nothing more irritating to the reader than having to go through a proposal containing a collage of different writing styles.

Cost Analysis

In developing cost estimates for the proposal, it is important that they be specific and realistic. State your underlying cost assumptions, and be firm about your estimates. Do not waffle in the realms of legalistic caveats. Keep in mind that, in many cases, your estimates are really starting points for final contract negotiations.

As stated previously, your proposal should have the lowest possible price since your competitors will attempt to do the same. Present your cost estimates in a clear and concise fashion. Use of spreadsheets for cost estimates is highly recommended. There are several spreadsheets that are widely used for costing. The advantage of using spreadsheets is that they allow you to fine tune your cost figures without re-calculating every item.

If you have an idea of the upper limit of the project cost based on budgetary constraints, the spreadsheet can define the upper limit, while you determine the most efficient unit costs and manpower requirements. You can change any one line item and see its impact on the bottom line immediately. This "what if?" feature is valuable for calculating the optimum levels of manpower and expenses within budgetary constraints.

Be realistic in determining your cost versus the scope of work required in the RFP. The following example illustrates the point:

A consulting firm was invited to compete on a proposal to the Indonesian government to develop and design several hazardous waste treatment facilities. The scope required the winning team to conduct environmental impact studies at several locations in Indonesia. The project was funded by a U.S. government grant administered by the US Embassy in Jakarta. The total approved budget was $100,000 – hardly enough to complete all the tasks demanded by the local government. This was to be a fixed price lump sum contract.

As soon as the consultant arrived in Jakarta, the first thing he did was set up an appointment with the economic attaché at the Embassy who was responsible for funding the project. The attaché told the consultant in no uncertain terms that the budgeted amount was fixed and that there would be no additional funds available to support this project. In other words, change orders are out of the question.

Based on this high quality information, the consultant submitted a proposal that spelled out clearly what his firm could do within that limited budget and nothing more. He knew full well that his firm ran the risk of losing the contract for being "non-responsive" to the terms of the RFP.

His competitors, on the other hand, all submitted proposals that promised to do everything the RFP called for with the "hope" of additional money being made available to them through change orders. They did not know that there was no more money to be had on that project. They had low-quality information.

Since the contract was a fixed price project, the firm that was awarded the job eventually lost millions of dollars trying to finish the project without the benefit of new infusion of funds from the client. The firm was not allowed to leave the country until the job was completed in accordance with the $100,000 contract.

Murphy's Law

Murphy's Law is alive and well when it comes to proposal preparation. If something can go wrong, it will. Always backup your working drafts on another computer or on a separate hard drive.

In addition to backing up all the computer files, you should also have another computer on standby. That doesn't mean you have to have two computers; it means you should know where you can gain access to a backup computer the moment something goes wrong with your computer. Deadlines have been missed because of computer malfunctions.

This is the primary reason why you should plan to complete your proposal at least 48 hours before the deadline. If something goes awry in the final production, you still have time to salvage the operation.

Anatomy of a successful proposal

A Fortune 500 company wanted to outsource the operation of its waste water treatment plant to a third party. It also wanted to reduce its debts on its balance sheet. So it issued a RFP to several large engineering companies to submit proposals to buy the treatment plant from the company, lease it back to the company and operate it on its behalf.

The firm that won the job did the following:

It met with the client's environmental manager and listened attentively to what his concerns were and the underlying reason for the RFP. The manager specifically stated in the RFP that terms such as "uniquely qualified" and "full service" were not to be used in the proposal.

It requested permission from the client to collect representative waste water samples from the plant in order to be able to do its own bench scale fine tune studies. This was not specifically required in the RFP. The fact that the firm took the trouble at its own expense to collect the samples and do the treatability tests was a critical factor in its being selected. It demonstrated to the client that the engineering firm was careful and deliberate in its approach to the proposal. Best of all, it gave the client a significant level of comfort that the firm would be able to treat the waste water based on its own tests and not on the historical effluent data provided by the client.

It provided a detail financial projection on how much money the client was going to save over the next 10 years. It met with the client's Chief Financial Officer several times just to make sure that he was comfortable with the numbers.

It offered performance guarantee and indemnification to the client for any violations that might occur for the duration of the contract. This satisfied the concerns from the client's legal counsel.

It reviewed its own projected monthly operating budget with the client to reassure the client that the plant would be staffed adequately. The client also wanted to make sure the firm would make a reasonable profit. The client was looking for stability in the future. The last thing it wanted was for the firm to abandon the project half way through because it failed to make a profit. For this project to be successful, it would have to be a win-win situation for both parties.

The successful firm went over and above the requirements of the RFP to reassure the client that it had done its homework and it had the ability to carry out the mission. It touched all bases: engineering, financial and legal.

Reassurance was paramount to the client because this is the first outsource/lease-back project it had ever done. The firm recognized the client's "internal politics" during its first meeting with the client's environmental manager and correctly focused on it.

The other firms that were invited to submit bids all sent in boilerplate type proposals. None of them requested actual waste water samples from the client. In fact, they all included a disclaimer that their proposed operational plans and costs were contingent on the accuracy of the client's own waste water effluent data. Instead of demonstrating confidence in their own ability to do the work, these firms opted to cover themselves with legalese and caveats. That did not give the client a sufficient level of comfort to award them the job.

Of course, all of these firms – with the exception of the winning firm – said in their proposals that they were "full service" and "uniquely qualified" to do the job. Evidently they never paid any attention to the RFP!

Chapter 11: How to Protect Your Proposal

There are unscrupulous buyers out there who would ask you to prepare a detailed technical proposal for them and yet they have no intention of hiring you. They may want to use your proposal to "shop around" and to solicit better prices from other consultants. This is totally unethical. Or they may just be looking for free advice. Or they may use your proposal as a bargaining tool during negotiation with the regulatory agency in order to get a better outcome. That too is unethical.

The best way to deal with these unethical non-buyers is to make sure that your proposal is copyrighted under U.S. Copyright law. Be sure to include the © symbol as a footer on every page of your proposal similar to the following.

Copyright © 2012 COPYRIGHT your firm's name. All Rights Reserved.

Also include a Confidentiality Statement in your proposal similar to the following paragraph:

"This proposal contains confidential and copyrighted proprietary commercial information and has been prepared solely for review and consideration by the staff of XYZ Corp. for the purpose of selecting a consulting team. Sharing the contents of this proposal with third parties - especially competing consultants - is strictly prohibited with our written consent."

Although your proposal is under copyright protection the moment it is created, it is a good idea to also register it with the U.S. Copyright Office in case you wish to bring a lawsuit for infringement of your proposal. Another benefit is that you will have the facts of their copyright on the public record and have a certificate of registration. You register your copyright by mailing a copy of it to the U.S. Copyright Office.

According to the Copyright Office, registered works may also be eligible for statutory damages and attorney's fees if you are successful in your litigation against anyone who violates your copyright. Finally, if registration occurs within 5 years of publication, it is considered prima facie evidence in a court of law. Go to the Copyright Office's website at www.copyright.gov for additional information.

Here is a case study: A client contacted the consultant by phone and asked the consultant to prepare a detailed proposal on how to set up an Environmental Management System. The client told the consultant that this was a sole source solicitation. No other proposals are being requested from other firms. The consultant spent a week preparing the proposal and sent it to the client. Every page of the proposal had a copyright insignia on it and there was also a Confidentiality Notice advising the client that information contained in the proposal was proprietary and that sharing of such information was strictly prohibited.

Two weeks later, the client called the consultant and told him that they had decided to issue a RFP to solicit more bids and that the consultant would be invited to rebid the job. When the RFP arrived at the consultant's office, he discovered that it contained his original proposal - word for word. The client awarded the contract to a firm with a lower price than the original unsolicited proposal.

The consultant filed a civil suit in Federal Court against the client for copyright infringement and unjust enrichment. The client settled the claim out of court.

Chapter 12: Working With Regulatory Agencies

As a consultant, you are often required to represent your clients before regulatory agencies. You may be preparing a permit for your client and you will have to meet with someone within an agency.

Being able to work effectively with the regulatory agencies is a critical element in any consultant's qualification.  If you have a cordial and professional working relationship with the agencies, you are more than halfway there. Many companies will hire you mainly because you have a reputation of being able to work effectively with the agency. They will hire you so that you can help them get the permits that they need in a timely manner.

On the other hand, if your approach is to constantly maintain an adversarial or antagonistic relationship with the agencies, you will be spending much of your valuable time and your client's money on a rather unproductive endeavor.

Here are some practical and "field-tested" pointers on how you can develop a professional and effective working relationship with the regulatory agencies.

1. Do your homework. You should always research the problem areas or issues that you want to get resolved with the agency. Check to see if there are any specific considerations that should be brought up. See if another company has resolved a similar problem with the same agency and find out what the solution is.

You should also research any applicable precedents outside of your agency's jurisdiction that may be pertinent to your case so that you can share them with the agency. What you are doing here is in effect giving the agency a certain level of comfort in knowing that other agencies have resolved similar issues in the manner you suggest. You are giving the folks at the agencies coverage.

2. Make a point of meeting the agency staff before you submit your client's permit application. Lay out your preferred approach and get to know the "case worker" or permit writer who will be handling your application. Always try to make a point of paying a courtesy "get-to-know-you" kind of visit. At the very least, phone the person at the agency and introduce yourself. In many cases, you will be pleasantly surprised by how cooperative the agency staff can be. Keep in mind that it is also to the agency's advantage to work things out amiably with your client. A professional working relationship with your client through you can and will save them time as well. Try to deal with the agency staff from their perspective. In other words, try to put yourself in their shoes.

3. Never attack the agency's regulations in front of the agency staff - no matter how you personally feel about the regulations. It does not matter how nonsensical you may feel about those regulations. Keep your personal opinion to yourself. Remember that it is the agency's job to enforce the regulations. If you don't like a particular set of environmental regulations, the time to make your point is during the promulgation (public comment) process. Attacking the agency staff will not enhance your working relationship one iota. All you are doing is antagonizing the staff and it will work

against your final objective – resolution of an issue you have before the agency. Remember this one too - the agencies have the laws that you don't like on their side and you don't.

4. You can (and often should) challenge the regulations and argue your case with your "case worker". State your case clearly and objectively. And again make sure you don't make it personal. Remember this – everything is negotiable (both sides can win in a negotiated settlement). But as soon as you make it personal, the issue rapidly degenerates into a zero-sum game (allowing one winner and one loser.) You want to avoid any needless confrontation as much as possible because more often than not you will end up being the loser.

Here is a true story: One Fortune 500 Company had a wastewater discharge permit problem before the regulatory agency in Puerto Rico. The plant manager decided to hire a local consultant who was very knowledgeable about the technical issues and the local regulations. Unfortunately this consultant also held some very strong personal views about the regulations and he took it upon himself on numerous occasions to express his personal views about the regulations and the agency staff who enforced them.

He told the staff that they were stupid and ignorant to be enforcing such bad regulations – at face-to-face meetings with the agencies! This apparently went on for several months and the permit application went absolutely nowhere. The company's environmental manager finally got suspicious of the delay and contacted the agency directly. The permit writer told the manager that the consultant was verbally abusive to the agency staff on many occasions and that they had refused to work with him. In fact, the consultant was ejected from the agency several times for being too abusive. The manager got on the next flight to Puerto Rico and fired the local consultant on the spot and replaced him with a much more personable and equally competent consultant. The relationship between the company and the agency took a dramatic turn for the better. But the company lost many months in the permitting process due to the inability of the first consultant to work with the agency.

Any smart future client will make sure that the consultant he hires knows how to represent him before a government agency. He will make sure the consultants have the right temperament.

If there is a deliverable involved, you might want to bounce the draft off the agency staff informally (in a face-to-face meeting if possible) before you submit it for your client formally. Some agencies like that idea - especially if you have established some sort of rapport with the staff. This approach gives them a chance to preview what is coming down the pike. Often times they will give you some timesaving suggestions that you can incorporate into your final application. It saves them time in reviewing your final product. This is a classic case of two parties working symbiotically towards a win-win solution.

Always submit your client's applications or documents to the agency on time. It is a matter of common courtesy to deliver what you promise in a timely manner. After all, if you expect your client to pay you on time, you should deliver your service on time too.

Never miss a deadline that you have agreed to with an agency. Why? Because it makes the agency look bad if you fail to deliver on time. More important, it makes the person who negotiated the agreement with you look bad.

Work across the table and solicit suggestions from the agency. There have been numerous instances when an agency official would go out of his way to help a consultant by suggesting different approaches to the problem at hand. This happens only when the official has trust and rapport with the consultant.

The bottom line of all of this is very simple. Treat agency personnel the same way you would like to be treated – with courtesy and professionalism. Since you expect to be paid on time, you should expect the agency to want to receive your reports on time. Experience shows that this common sense management approach goes a long way.

And if you do a great job representing your clients, you will get lots of repeat business.

Chapter 13: Thirteen Common Mistakes Made by Consultants

A recent survey of buyers of professional services shows that 85% of buyers have encountered major problems with a consultant during the sales process. The top three problems are:

They don't listen to me

They didn't understand my needs.

They didn't respond to my requests in a timely manner.

The following are 13 common mistakes made by consultants in their daily dealings with their existing and future clients.

These consultants are most likely your competitors. So learn from their mistakes and benefit from their self-imposed misfortunes.

Mistake #1: Fail to Return All Phone Calls Promptly

There are two kinds of consultants: Those who return clients' phone calls promptly and those who don't. The

ones who return phone calls in a timely manner are generally a lot more successful.

Unfortunately, many consultants fall into the second category. In this electronic age of pagers, cellular phones, blackberries, iPad and email, there is absolutely no excuse whatsoever for anyone in the consulting business not to return phone calls from their clients within 24 hours.

You should always be responsive and return phone calls - no matter how busy you are. If you have to call your future client and tell him that you are too busy to talk to him at length, do it. Just set up a more convenient time with your client later. Your client will not be upset with the fact that you are too busy to discuss his case with you immediately. In fact, he will be very appreciative of the fact that you take the time out of your busy schedule just to return his phone call.

Let's see how long it takes to return a phone call even when you are "very busy". You pick up the phone and hit the return call button and say, "Hi...I am sorry I can't talk with you at length right now. I have a family emergency. I will call you tomorrow morning. Thanks."

It takes a grand total of 15 seconds! Are you really THAT busy that you can't take 15 seconds to return a client's phone call?

Returning phone calls promptly is just basic good business common sense – not to mention professional courtesy. However, it is amazing how many consultants fail to return their future clients' phone calls in a timely manner. Incidentally, the bigger the consulting firm, the slower it is for the firm to return phone calls. Many firms have lost potentially lucrative contracts because of this bad habit.

In a recent 60-Minutes TV interview, the most successful professional football agent in the National Football league (NFL) Drew Rosenhaus says he takes his clients' phone calls 24/7 - in the showers, in the middle of the night, and when he was on a date. He has 170 clients and he is the most successful agents in the NFL. He never misses his clients' phone calls. Here is a direct quote from Rosenhaus on 60 Minutes: "If I get a call in the middle of the night, I have to take it. If I'm with a girl I have to take it. If I'm in the shower, I have to take it."

There are over 1000 agents in the NFL. Over 80% of his clients came from other agents. His dedication to his football player clients is legendary and he was the inspiration behind the Tom Cruise hit movie Jerry Maguire.

Another classic example follows:

A wastewater treatment plants had a particularly challenging problem with a fecal coliform issue a number of years ago. The environmental manager contacted a consultant in a large "full service" consulting firm (the 95-30-5 type) and left several messages requesting the professional services of an experienced sanitary engineer to go to the plant to diagnose the problem. One full week later – the consultant called back and told the client that he had sent out broadcast emails and voice mail messages to all the key managers conveying the request and did not get a single reply back from any of his colleagues. This is a leading ENR 50 firm with over 10,000 engineers and scientists! They failed to make the connection and lost a great business opportunity.

If you are a large firm, you want to make sure that your staff does not operate as a group of individual consultants doing their own thing. In many ways, these big firms operate much like a one-person firm. The individual consultants all have voice mail and many of them work out of their homes. The only difference is cost to the future clients. These big firms have much larger multipliers and overhead. That's fine as long as these are value added services. Your future clients would (or should) expect significant amount of synergy and interaction among the 10,000 consultants in these large firms that will result in an exceptionally high quality of service to justify the higher rates. Very often that is not the case.

Remember - you cannot make a sale if your staff does not return your future clients' phone messages or emails.

Here is a test. Have someone outside your firm make a service request call to your receptionist and see how long it takes for someone within your firm to call back.

Mistake #2: Change Orders

Many consultants come in low on their budget in their proposal with the full expectation of issuing change orders later.

That is a bad mistake. The old trick of "getting your foot in the door" first does not work anymore.

Unless there are strong extenuating circumstances (such as your client requesting additional work from you), you should avoid change orders at all costs because it sends a very negative message to your clients. It says basically two things. One, the job was not priced out properly by you and now your client has to go to his boss and ask for more money for you. Second impression is that you got the job by low-balling. Neither scenario presents a pretty picture from the standpoint of your client.

Change orders make your client look very bad within his. Many companies consider change orders as cost overrun. And your client's internal problem worsens if the change order value exceeds his internal budget. Your change order also means additional paper work for your busy client who now has to justify your change order to his management. He has to explain to his management why the work wasn't budgeted properly in the first place.

Remember: It was your client who accepted your original budget. Now your change order puts him in a very awkward position within his organization.

Remember the old adage about General Motors? What's good for General Motor is good for the country. Well, what's bad for your client is bad for you.

Moral of the story is that you should always look at the job from your client's perspective. Try to understand the internal politics your client faces within his organization. If he has to navigate through a mine field of rules and procedures to get your hired in the first place, you are not going to make his job any easier by coming up with change orders.

Always look out for your client's interest - it will pay big in dividends later.

It pays dividends later if you tell your client the hard truth about the true cost of the job up front. Look at it this way, if a client is only interested in doing every job on the cheap, maybe you don't want him as a client anyway. It pays to be up front with your client on cost. Don't try to low-ball the project.

Always insists on your fair and reasonable fees. It is often counterproductive to give instant discount on your professional rates. Why? Because it discounts your reputation; it cheapens your value to your clients. If you drop your fees to "match" your competitor's just to get the job, your client is going to think why your rate was so high in the first place.

In sum, the old practice of low-balling to get your foot in the door does not work any more. It just alienates your clients.

Mistake #3: Wanting Extra for High Quality Product

Many "full service and uniquely qualified" consulting firms include in their proposals a significant portion of fees dedicated to "senior review".

Try to look at this approach for a minute - from the perspective of your future client. Senior Review is the charge you want your future client to pay to have some vice president in your firm review the work of a "uniquely qualified" consultant who is already billed to your client at $200 an hour!

What kind of message are you sending out to your client?

It tells your future client that perhaps the $200 an hour "uniquely qualified" consultant is not quite so unique or qualified after all if his work needs to be checked by a more senior person at $300 an hour. Quality assurance costs should be part of your overhead. It is your cost of doing business. Without quality assurance, a consulting firm will not be in business for very long. You would no more charge your future client extra for this than you would bill him extra for the use of your office furniture. It should be part of your overhead.

Unfortunately, this practice is used all too commonly to increase the billable rate of many senior administrative persons on the consulting firm's overhead staff. This practice may keep your accountants happy in the short run. But at the end of the day, it is your future clients that really matter.

Mistake # 4: Fail to Learn Your Trade

Don't ask your client to pay you to learn about your business. Keep in mind that she will be paying for it through your overhead and multiplier. It is a bad mistake to ask your client to pay for it twice.

A major multinational consulting firm went to a manufacturing plant and requested time to put on a meeting to brief the plant manager and his staff on how to obtain a new air permit from the state agency. At the end of the meeting, the manager requested a written proposal from the consultants.

In the proposal, about 20 percent of the total cost was dedicated to time spent by the consultants to learn about the procedures for obtaining the air permits. They allotted a significant number of hours in the proposal to familiarize themselves with the applicable state regulations. This was after they had told their clients at the sales meeting that they were the nation's foremost experts on air permits! And now they wanted their future clients to pay for their staff's learning experience.

This is a classic case of consultants wanting to be paid while they learn on the job.

To make matters worse, these consultants also proposed to charge the client 4 hours of a secretary's time at $35 an hour to "make arrangement" for photocopying the permit application. This was not the cost of photocopying - but the cost for "arranging" for photocopying. Actual photocopying costs were extra.

When the plant manager rejected the firm's proposal, the consultants invoiced the plant for time spent on the sales meeting.

The invoice was never paid. And the consultants were never hired on any other job either.

Below is a very peculiar posting on LinkedIn by a environmental and safety consultant frantically looking for help. He billed himself as a consultant and yet he was unable to find a common set of standards commonly used by consultants in their profession. He also mis-named the standards as ISO 18001. It should have been OHSAS 18001. On top of that, he was looking for someone to email him a copyrighted document illegally.

LinkedIn is an business connection network used by millions of people worldwide. He posted his full name and his company's name for millions to see.

Another consultant posted the following message on LinkedIn - bad grammar and all:

> "I have MS in Environmental engineering.
>
> As far as experience,i dont have any,But i feel confident in doing this job. my company is a very small one with 7 employees.as far as training is concerned,no training is provided to me.i just have to review the previous reports,understand it and write a report based on the site conditions and other data.final correction is made by my boss before sending to the client".

This recent college graduate with zero years of experience and training was looking for help in writing a Health and Safety Plan.

His company - an environmental consulting firm in New York - bills this neophyte out to clients as a Project Manager!

Mistake # 5: Prepare Dishonest Proposals

In your zeal to win a contract, make sure you do not overly inflate your firm's qualifications and experience in the proposal. Unfortunately, many consultants fall into that trap. See the following case history:

A company issued a Request for Proposal to several engineering firms to design a 2 million gallons a day (mgd) advanced wastewater treatment plant for one of its manufacturing facilities. One of the prerequisites clearly stated in the RFP was that the consultants must have had actual design experience on treatment plants of comparable capacities.

An engineering firm came back with a proposal that clearly claimed that it had designed a 4 mgd plant for a particular food processing plant. It made the representation that it had the requisite experience as stated in the RFP.

The client took the liberty of calling the food processing plant to check on the engineering firm's claim. It turned out that this design firm never designed such a treatment plant. In turned our that the firm's entire experience consisted of several graduate students working part-time on a wastewater treatability study that resulted in a conceptual design of a treatment plant that was much smaller in scale than 2 million gallons per day. It was only 200,000 gallons per day - one-tenth the size.

When the client confronted this engineering firm with this fact, the response was that they must have made a typographical error in the proposal! The problem was that this particular "typo" appeared in four different places in the proposal in both narrative and tabular forms.

This design firm made false claim in the proposal and when exposed tried to blame it on the secretarial help.

Not a good start to try to win a contract.

Many consultants also pad their resumes in their proposals. This is not a good idea. Your future client will spot the exaggerations and out right lies in a minute. There are consultants who claim to have 15 years of consulting experience when they are not more 30 years old.

Once a client doubts the veracity of your experience and qualifications, he is going to have questions about everything you say in your proposal. Credibility is like virginity, once lost it is gone forever.

Mistake # 6: Fail to Project a Positive and Right Image

Many consultants fall into the trap of spending too much time talking about themselves - often to their own detriment. Remember this: Marketing gets you in front of the client and nothing more. It is selling that will get you the job.

The stereotypical image of a super salesman as a slick smooth talker is a relic of the past. In fact, surveys after surveys have demonstrated that the top sales people are the ones who possess excellent listening skills. They let their customers talk 60 to 70 percent of the time. They wait to offer solutions or products to their customers only after they have listened and fully understood their customer's needs and concerns.

Before you have the slightest chance of landing a contract, you must understand your future client's problem. The trick of the trade is a six-letter word - listen. Think about this. If you have a physical ailment and need medical help, would you go to see a doctor who keeps telling you how great he is and how many post-graduate degrees he received from some ivy-league medical school? The only way a doctor can understand his patient's ailment is to listen to the patient's complaint. The consultants are doctors. The future clients are patients.

An effective and successful consultant always listens to his client's problems. He listens before he talks. A smart consultant focuses on his future client's needs - not on how great he is or how wonderful his consulting firm is. He listens. He analyzes his client's problems carefully. And then he comes up with a cost-effective solution. After all, remember that's what your future client wants first and foremost from you - a cost-effective solution.

It was President Abraham Lincoln who said: "People don't care how much you know until they know how much you care."

Remember that your future clients could care less about your past history as long as they feel comfortable that you can do the job for them. They could care less about how great you were, how great your company is. Your clients want one thing and one thing only. They want you to fix their problems. They are looking for the individuals who can solve their problems for them. The name of your firm matters a lot less to your clients than the person assigned to the job.

You are NOT trying to convince your client to buy your services. In your sales pitch, you are in effect trying to give your client reasons to select you. It is a proven fact that people buy for emotional reasons and justify their decision later intellectually.

Establish and maintain a positive attitude in your dealings with your clients. No one likes a doomsayer. People like to deal with other folks with positive attitudes.

One of the things you should never do is bad mouth or rundown your competition. It projects a very unprofessional image. If you should lose in a bid to your competitor, do not react by saying uncomplimentary things about the winner. Aside from projecting the image of a sore loser, you are also challenging the decision of your future client. You are in effect telling your future client that he has made the wrong decision by not selecting you.

When your future client tells you that he is awarding the job to another firm, your proper reaction should be as follows:

"I am sorry to hear that we are not successful. Can you tell us where we could have done a better job in our proposal?"

After your client debriefs you (and many of them will do that if you approach them in a positive manner), you should end the conversation or meeting with something like:

"Well, thanks again for the opportunity to bid on the project. We appreciate it very much even though we are not successful this time. I want to especially thank you for your feedback. It will help us quite a bit. We wish you all the best on this new project. If there is anything we can do for you in the future, please don't hesitate to let us know."

Your client has just done you a great favor by giving you feedback on why you were not successful. Take heed of what the client tells you and thank him profusely again. This is how you learn.

You will be amazed how often the same client would call you back later if his relationship with your competitor should go sour. Or maybe he will contact you when another opportunity comes up again.

Never be a sore loser and never bad mouth your competition in front of your future clients.

Mistake #7: Fail to Maintain a Personal Touch

In his book "The Pursuit of Wow!" best selling author and management consultant Tom Peters (co-author of In Search of Excellence) talks about the value and impact of sending handwritten "thank-you" notes to customers. This old personal touch carries enormous weight especially in these days of computer automation. It takes less than one minute to write that note. And it will reap big dividends in return.

Jack Welch, the former Chairman and CEO of General Electric - the world's largest industrial conglomerate – is famous for scribbling personal notes to his staff.

According to a June 8th, 1998 article in Newsweek Magazine, Jack Welch's "handwritten notes sent to everyone from direct reports to hourly workers possess enormous impact". They have been described as intimate and spontaneous. This is just another example of the power of personal notes.

A corporate manager used to get many Christmas cards from prospective consulting firms. He always grouped them into two piles. The first pile contained pre-printed company cards but with short handwritten personal notes addressed to him. This was always a small pile. The second pile contained pretty cards with pre-printed company names (with no signature) that came in labeled envelopes. There was always a big pile. Guess which pile he tossed out every year.

It is amazing how many consulting firms go through the expenses of printing up beautiful greeting cards and not taking the time (one minute per client per year!) to scribble a few personal notes to their customers and future clients! Here is a quote Tom Peters' book "The Pursuit of Wow": "A two-line, largely unreadable scrawl beats a page and a half spit out by the laser printer." Tom Peter's book "The Pursuit of Wow!" is an excellent source of inspiration on good customer service.

Remember - People don't forget kindness. The converse is equally true. They appreciate the little personal touches. Always treat your clients the way you would like to be treated.

A critical point to remember:

Always be nice and courteous to your future clients' administrative assistants. They hold the key to your client's doorway. Many of them screen their bosses' emails and phone calls. They set their bosses' meeting schedules. They can get you in the door or they can keep you out.

They are the true gate keepers of your clients.

If you are ever discourteous or rude to these folks, may the Almighty have mercy on you. You will never be connected to your future clients.

Mistake #8: Lack of Passion

Chances are that your future client gets an average of two calls a week from your competitors all claiming to be the best, the most uniquely qualified, and the most comprehensive full service consulting firm ever imagined in mankind.

So what is going to set you apart from this crowd?

You want to make sure that when your staff meets with the client, they understand their own work and capability and more important they actually believe in their work.

If your staff does not project an image of self-confidence, no one is going to hire them. There is nothing more irritating to your future client if he senses that your staff does not even believe in their own sales pitch.

This is an area where smaller firms do a lot better than the large ones for the simple reason that there is better internal communication within small consulting firms. If you fit in this category, take full advantage of it. This is your strongest selling point as far as your future clients are concerned.

Every consultant should be able to articulate in 20 to 30 seconds what he does for a living and the benefits he can bring to his clients. People call this the elevator pitch - something you tell people in the same elevator in between floors.

Consider the following examples:

"Hello – I am Bob Jones. I am an environmental engineer with a company called Wastewater Inc. We improve plant performance and save money for our clients."

"Hi – My name is Jane Smith. I am a hydrogeologist with Groundwater Inc. We help our clients clean up their contaminated ground water. My job is to find out the extent of the contamination and recommend remedial alternatives to our clients."

Both of these examples offer the client a clear picture of what the consultants do and also the benefits they provide to their clients. All in under 30 seconds.

Here is something you can do in your company: At your next staff meeting, ask each member of your staff to stand up and say in 40 words or less or under 30 seconds what your firm does and why it does it so well. Whether it is true or not is unimportant. The main thing is that you want to make sure your staff believes in it.

Drew Rosenhaus - the legendary NFL agent - is exemplary in his passion and commitment to his clients; He views his clients as his family. Here is a direct quote from him on TV: "I live it, eat it, sleep it every single minute of the day......it is not like a job...it is fun".

You can't ask for more from a consultant.

Mistake #9: Fail to Provide Service with a Smile

A lot of people talk about world-class service. Just exactly what is world class service?

If you have ever taken an oversea Business Class flight on Singapore Airlines overseas, you will understand what real world class service means.

The minute you get on board the aircraft, you notice that you are being noticed. The attendants know you by name without having to read from a passenger list in their hands. They serve you drinks without being too intrusive. They anticipate your every need. If you should fall asleep, they make sure you are covered up with a blanket – without ever waking you up.

Their mission is very simple. They want to make sure you remember the way you have been treated on board so that you will fly with them again on your next trip.

The passenger service on this airline is so exemplary that it trains many North American airlines that sorely need such training.

This kind of world-class service can be a model for consultants.

Another model is a famous retail tire chain store. This company offers excellent free service to walk-in customers. If you get a nail in your tire, the technician at this store will patch it up for you – absolutely free of charge. How can they afford that? It is a safe bet that many of the grateful walk-ins will end up purchasing brand new tires from this chain some time later.

This is the reason many attorneys offer free initial consultation. They are betting that some of the recipients of the free consultation will return later as paying clients.

Offering free service or advice It is a very effective way to generate good will and new business. Check out your own service to see if it matches up to the examples above.

Mistake #10: Promising Too Much and Delivering Less

In their eagerness to win the job, many consultants tend to make promises that they cannot keep and end up delivering less. That is a recipe for disaster.

Be very careful with your clients about deadlines. Do not assume that just because you think you are giving your client a quality product, it will not matter to him if the product is two weeks late.

Consider this scenario: Your client has a building site that is contaminated. His company needs desperately to build a factory on that site to meet their customers' demands. You promise your client you are going to be able to finish cleaning up his contaminated site by June if you are awarded the job even though you know it is a very tight schedule. But since the client is in a hurry and you want the job, you decide to stick with that tight schedule. You tell yourself that maybe everything will fall into place and you will meet your self-imposed deadline.

Based on your promise to him, your client tells his production people they can expect construction to start in August and completion by next May. Production planning is now underway for that new factory. Senior management is now counting on millions of dollars of future revenue from this new factory once it is built.

You have now been awarded the job based on your promise of early completion. But everything has not fallen into place as you had hoped. There is no way you can meet your June deadline. You now have to go to see your client in May and tell him it will take another 3 months to finish cleaning that site.

How do you think your client is going to react to your bad news?

Not only have you delivered less than you promised, you have also committed the cardinal sin of making your client look bad within his organization.

A better way to handle this situation would be to be realistic about the schedule in your proposal and in the interview. It would be better to lose the job and maintain your reputation with the client for future jobs than to make a promise that you cannot keep.

Here is another example:

A consultant from a national firm stopped by a waste water treatment plant in Puerto Rico to discuss the concept of outsourcing the operation and maintenance of the plant.

During the discussion, the company told the consultant that the largest budgeted item was sludge hauling and disposal. Upon hearing this, the consultant immediately launched into his sales pitch about how great his sister company was in managing waste solids and that he would have the Regional Vice President call the client right away.

Two weeks went by before this Vice President called the client and offered him his services – without ever asking the clients once about their requirements.

A better way to handle this situation would be to ask some key questions regarding the client's needs and/or call him yourself to gather additional information regarding his needs and then connect him with the right technical person in your organization. It is critical for you to follow through with these technical people to make sure they contact your clients.

Always keep your promise to your future clients.

Mistake# 11: Fail to Keep Their Existing Clients Happy

Research has repeatedly shown that consultants lose more existing clients from benign neglect than from any other single cause.

Never take your existing clients for granted. You do so at your own peril.

It is absolutely imperative that you nurture the relationship. Remember, it costs a lot more - 6 times more costly - to develop new clients than to maintain existing ones. It just makes good economic sense to keep your existing clients happy.

Yet unbelievably, there was a consultant who failed to return her existing client's urgent phone call because she did not think it was important enough. She was busy doing something else. It was her biggest client who called. The client had an urgent consulting assignment for her to do – without any need for her to prepare a proposal - and she lost the opportunity by not returning the call. Worse yet, she tried to argue with her client that although she did not return his call, she did send him an email. That was not the case either. She didn't. She was one of those people who just have to have the last words in any discussions. By her own ineptitude, she lost a steady client who had given her small company well over $500,000 in consulting contracts – all without having to write a single proposal.

After you get the job, you need to make sure the consultants assigned to the new project have some marketing acumen. Every time they interact with your client, they are representing your company. Your client views your company through the consultants you send them.

It is generally a good practice to establish open dialog with your clients. Some consulting firms assign their senior managers to act as client liaisons to ensure good customer relations. That is a very good approach. What you want to do is to be able to say to your client: "Look, let me be the first one to know if we mess up on your project. Here is my office number, my home number, my cell phone and my pager. Call me any time you think you have a problem with our service." Nine times out of ten, you will not get a call at all. But when you do get that call, respond to it immediately after **listening** carefully to the complaint.

Poor customer relations will do great harm to your existing business. It never fails. Consider the case of two dive operations in Bonaire – a scuba divers' paradise. These two dive operations are located right next to each other. One dive operation has dive instructors that are friendly, happy and more than willing to help their customers. The operation next door is a very well established operation on the island. It had a stellar reputation.

Unfortunately the management there has become complacent and neglected its customers. That attitude permeates through the entire organization - as it always does. The staff members there are surly and rude to their paying customers. They just stop caring whether their customers are having a good time or not. This negative attitude shows through and their customers see it – loud and clear. After several years of neglect, the second dive operation has lost most of its customers to the first one.

Here is something you can do. Make a list of all your clients, call a fourth of them each week and see how well things are coming along. Are they happy with your staff's work? When you get to the bottom of the list, start all over again.

Mistake #12: Fail to Do Those Little Things

Make sure your receptionist answers phone calls promptly and meets visitors (a.k.a. future clients) with courtesy. Keep in mind that your receptionist is your company. She represents you. She is the first impression your future client has about your company. She is the first line of contact when the outside world comes in.

It is absolutely critical that you train your front line troops (including receptionists) in the proper way of answering phone calls from future clients. Below is a case in point:

A computer service company asks its customers to bring in their computers for repairs between the hours of 8 and 10 am. And yet, all of its service representatives attend daily staff meetings from 8 to 8:30. So no one is available to help any future or existing clients who happen to walk in during this time slot. The net result, it keeps 4 to 5 different customers waiting for 30 minutes every day. That's a potential loss of 1,250 customers over a year period! How many firms can sustain this magnitude of loss?

In this case, the receptionist saves the day. She is prompt in paging the service reps and conscientious in making sure the reps respond to her page. This reinforces the point made earlier that the receptionist is the ambassador of a service-oriented business.

She would page the service rep as soon as a customer shows up. If the service rep has not appeared in two minutes, she pages him again with the comment "Please come to the reception area immediately – you have a customer waiting for you!" She repeats the announcement until he shows up. That takes some of the sting out of waiting.

It is not uncommon for a future client to call into a big consulting firm and be transferred from one person to the next and the next with nothing more than a "hold on" – if at all. It is like a relay race with no end in sight! Government agencies do that a lot. But now it is becoming more common in the private sector.

The proper and courteous way to handle this is to say the following: "Sorry I can't help you. But I would like to pass you on to someone who may be able to help you. She is in charge of the area you are interested in. Her name is Susan and her telephone extension is 2345 in case we get disconnected. Please hold on and I will connect you."

This takes all but less than one minute to do.

A referral like that can sure make a positive first impression on your future client. We all know from daily personal experience just how critical first impression is. The same holds for your clients.

Mistake #13: Fail to Deal with Complaints Promptly

If your client comes to you with a problem, deal with it immediately. Do not let it fester. You should always treat the problem the same way you treat a small tumor in your brain. Check it out immediately. See if it is malignant. Early detection can save you from losing your client.

The best way to deal with this is to listen (here is that word again) - listen to your client's problem. Do not become defensive. Listen to the problem carefully. In many cases, the perceived problem is just that - some sort of misunderstanding between your staff and your client. All that is required is a few phone calls to clear up the misunderstanding.

If you should find fault with your staff, deal with it right away, get to the root cause of it and make sure it does not happen again. More important – get back to the client and tell her what you have done. Many consultants fail to do that.

Always make a point of getting back to your client regarding the compliant - one way or the other. It is just common courtesy. If people take the time to bring a potential problem to your attention, they deserve a prompt feedback from you.

When you are handling the situation with your client, make sure you don't fall into the trap of showering him with platitudes. There is nothing more irritating to your client than to keep hearing you say that you are here to serve him and to make sure that his external requirements are being met – and then nothing happens.

Here is an example:

A client had problems with the sloppiness of calculations from a consulting engineer. He left a message with the engineer's supervisor. The next day the client received a call from the head of that consulting division who proceeded to say all the right things – "You are a very important client to us. What can we do to meet your expectations? We are dedicated to meeting your requirements."

The client told the senior consultant that all he needed to do was to either improve the firm's internal quality control procedures or assign another engineer to the project.

The consultant said he would look into it and get back to the client right away. Nothing happened. There was no follow up.

It turned out to be "all talk and no action".

The moral of this story is this: Always deliver what you say you are going to deliver. When your client has a problem, he wants action. This is not the time to be glib about it. He wants resolution immediately. All the platitudes in the world will not ease the client's anxiety.

Remember this: It is not what you say that matters. It is what you do that counts.

Additional References

The following are several extremely valuable resources that can help you make connections with your future clients.

Each of these books offers its own unique perspective on topics that have everything to do with customer service and common sense approach to business.

"The Pursuit of Wow" by Tom Peters.
Tom Peters reveals many little things that can make your business stand out from the crowd. A classic example he gives is to send your client a handwritten note instead of a laser jet printed memo. You just can't beat the personal touch.

The "I Hate Selling" by Allan S. Boress.
This book is written by a CPA who made a living teaching other CPAs how to keep their existing clients and how to get new ones. It has some very practical and down-to-earth advice for all professionals.

"Precision – A New Approach to Communication" by Michael McMaster and John Grinder.
This is NLP (Neurolinguistic Programming) applied in a business setting. It gives you numerous real life examples on how to obtain high quality information in a business meeting. It is amazing how much information you can get just by asking the right questions.

"The Professional Service Firm 50" by Tom Peters.
The ever engaging Tom Peters gives his no-holds barred advice on what you need to do to make your professional service firm GREAT! This is a must read for consultants.

"The Art of Plain Talk" by Rudolph Flesch.
This book shows you how to write in Plain English and how to avoid buzzwords. It has a readability scale you can apply to your writing.

"Moving Mountains – the Art of Letting Others See Things Your Way." By Henry Boettinger.
This is by far the best book on communication and presentation – bar none. It contains some of the best advice you will ever find on how to connect with your audience. If you are allowed to read only one book while marooned on a desert island, this is the one to read. Unfortunately, this book is out of print and is very difficult to find. Some local libraries have it.

"The Art of the Start" by Guy Kawasaki.
This book is for any business person or consultant who has the entrepreneurial spirit. Guy talks about the ten steps that someone should follow in order to get money from venture capitalists. Getting jobs from your future client is not that much different. He also gives excellent advice on how to make effective PowerPoint presentations and what not to do.

"The Power of Simplicity" by Jack Trout and Steve Rivkin.
This is an excellent book on how to keep your business simple. It gives many examples of why many companies failed because they tried to complicate their businesses. They quote Ralph Waldon Emerson: "Nothing is more simple than greatness. Indeed to be simple is to be great".

"Beyond Bullet Points" by Cliff Atkinson. Cliff is the foremost authority on how to simplify your PowerPoint presentations and avoid using those awful bullet points.

This book will show you how to tell your story to your clients and get them to listen to you. Try it his way and you will be amazed at the response from your audience.

"Made to Stick – why Some Ideas Survive and Others Die" by Chip Heath & Dan Heath. This book describes in great details the six basic elements that are needed for an idea to stick. The elements are: Simplicity, unexpectedness, concreteness, credibility, emotion and stories. Apply these elements in your sales approach and you will most likely succeed.

About the Author

Norman Wei has over 33 years of practical experience both as a consultant and corporate manager.

For nine years, from 1989 to 1998, Norman was the senior corporate environmental manager at Star-Kist Foods Inc. – then a subsidiary of the H.J. Heinz Company. As corporate manager, he awarded numerous professional service contracts to both large and small consulting firms. He reported directly to the Chief Financial Officer of the company.

He is now the principal and founder of Environmental Management and Training, LLC., a consulting firm based in Cape Coral, Florida. He has conducted over a hundred seminars.

He has been on both sides of the table - having hired and fired numerous consultants and being a consultant himself.

Norman Wei has authored numerous articles on business services and environmental management. He is the author of an article on "Winning Proposals" in the Architectural & Engineering Systems Journal. In July 1999, his landmark article on "Connecting with Your Future Clients" was published in Environmental Engineer.

Other business articles by Norman appear in the Wastebiz Magazine, Safety + Health (a National Safety Council publication), Industrial Safety & Hygiene, Water and Pollution Control, Business and Legal Reports, Pollution Engineering, Business and Legal Reports, The

Financial Post, Canadian Shipping and Marine Engineering, Water & Wastes Engineering, and Civic Public Works.

He has recently published a book on "Presentations that Work". It is available on Amazon.com. He writes a blog on "Excellence in Presentation" that has received over 140,000 hits.

Norman Wei serves on the editorial advisory board of Business and Legal Reports and is a contributing editor for Pollution Engineering Magazine.

Norman Wei holds a Master's Degree in Civil Engineering from the University of Toronto, Canada.

He now resides in Cape Coral, Florida.

In-House Seminars by Norman Wei

Norman Wei can come to your office and conference and deliver a customized in-house course for your staff at a very reasonable rate.

For more information, contact:

Norman Wei
P.O. Box 152239
Cape Coral, FL 33915

Telephone: 360-490-6828
Fax: 1-866-230-6280
Website: www.thegreatconsultants.com
Email: Norman@thegreatconsultants.com
Blog: www.nobullets.wordpress.com

www.ingramcontent.com/pod-product-compliance
Lightning Source LLC
Chambersburg PA
CBHW030925180526
45163CB00002B/464